A Life Lived on Riverview Lane

By

Jim

D0902216

Dedication

This book is dedicated in loving memory to my parents, Bill and Pat Huckaby. Thank you for teaching me respect, honesty, responsibility, discipline and the importance of hard work. Most of all, thank you for showing me love.

This book is also dedicated to my nephew, Demian Patterson who had a profound impact on my life.

I love you all and I think of you often.

Disclaimer

I would like to start out by saying that you are likely to find some misspellings and grammatical errors, as you are reading this book. Throughout this long two-year endeavor, there was an enormous amount of work that was put into writing this book. While editing the book, I corrected the errors, but because of a glitch in the computer program, it wouldn't save the corrections that were made. In the end, you are reading an imperfect book, written by an imperfect person with an imperfect computer program. If you are looking for perfection, you are likely to be disappointed. If you're looking for a genuine book written from the heart, then you will likely enjoy this book regardless of its imperfections. Happy reading.

Acknowledgements

I have a few people I would like to thank for making this book possible. First and foremost, I would like to thank my wife, Sherri. She has been a rock of support throughout this entire project. Thanks for all your patience, feedback and constructive criticism.

To my siblings, thank you for a lifetime of love and memories and thanks for allowing me to use my recollections of all of you in my book.

To my childhood friend Greg Collins, I would like to say thank you for your constant encouragement. Without your endless support, I would have never overcome my dyslexia and finally learned how to read. Greg recently said, "From where you came from, it's a small miracle that you would go on to write a book." I guess it speaks of the profound willpower of the human spirit.

To my friend of nearly 50 years, Chris Logan. Thank you for inspiring me to write these stories. Chris was there from day one of this project. This book would not have been possible without his unwavering encouragement and positive feedback.

A special thank you to all of my friends that are woven throughout the pages of this book. You guys have provided me with a lifetime of incredible memories.

Thanks to all of my friends and acquaintances that so graciously read my stories and provided so much support during the writing process of this book. I really appreciated the feedback from each and every one of you.

Last and certainly not least, I would like to thank God for giving me a life full of challenges, adversity, faith, hope and love, no matter how hard things may have gotten. Thank You for teaching me the true meaning of determination, patience and perseverance.

Most importantly, I am thankful to know a truly loving God. Life is good.

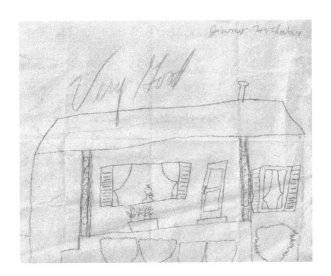

A Message from the Author

The book you are about to read only represents my account and perspective of the events that took place during my life. The stories are not meant to represent anyone else's views or opinions other than my own. Some of the names have been changed to protect the privacy of those written about.

Enjoy, Jimi Huckaby

Daddy, Biff, Mom, Jimi & Jerry: on the day of Dad's retirement from the Army 1967

Foreword

By Chris Logan

"I come from people who believe the home place is as vital and necessary as the beating of your own heart. It is that single house where you were born, where you lived out your childhood, where you grew into young manhood. It is your anchor in the world, that place, along with the memory of your kinsmen at the long supper table every night and the knowledge that it would always exist, if nowhere but in memory."

> Harry Crews from A Childhood: The Biography of a Place

The older I get, the more I contemplate the meaning of the word home. The word has to be up there with love and family on the "most important word in the world list." Has to be. Is. The saying "Home is where the heart" is rings true; however, it rings truer when emotions and place can interlock, when the word home is tangible and not just based in warm memories of a home. Few people get to reside in the same home for most of their life. Few people get to become a long-lasting part of a home- one home- as concrete and fixed as a joist or an eave. Few people get to go from childhood to adulthood, from child to caretaker, to husband with a new family under the same roof. I am not one of those people, but Jimi Huckaby is one of the lucky few who sits at that long supper table, in that same single house. Home.

As a high school English teacher, I am lucky enough to have reflective discussions with students. I am not trying to depress them, but sometimes our class discussions veer into very personal territory, such as the various meanings of home. Many of them, like me, do not have one single place to return to in the physical sense, a place that has always been there for them, a physical place where past, present, and future intermingle and provide a sort of timeless safety net. Home. My grandparents' houses have been sold, as has the place I called home throughout the majority of my childhood and a good share of my adulthood. Other families now live where many of my foundational experiences took place- I can no longer at will physically touch the walls that absorbed so much of my experiences, my family's experiences, me. I can only remember, and memories can't always be trusted. They can be felt, but can they be held, touched? Are they just fragments of something once whole? Do they stand as true as homes?

My childhood home, as fate would have it, was on Riverview Drive, the same street as Jimi's family. When we moved to Shepherdsville in the early 1970s, Jimi and I became fast friends, even though he was a few years older than me. He was an instrumental part of my childhood. Through him, over the years, I was exposed to silent movies, The Marx Brothers, Laurel and Hardy, Evel Knievel, and Cheap Trick, not to mention professional wrestling and camping out. My family owned a super 8 movie camera, and once Dad sold it to Jimi, we became child auteurs, making our own silent movies for over half a decade. As a kid, I loved going to Jimi's house. His parents were so kind to me, and his father made me laugh endlessly. We had an unbelievably rich childhood on Riverview Drive- precious memories I will never forget: drawing cartoons; filming movie scenes, including one that almost burned up the Huckaby backyard; making profanity laced party tapes; and listening to a vast array of classic rock. I spent many hours at the Huckaby household, and I am so glad that I was part of the tapestry, a small part, of his home.

After high school, I went off to the University of Kentucky and really never came back to my home, at least as a resident, on Riverview Lane. When Jimi and I reconnected a few years ago, both of us older and grayer, memories about our lives on that street poured out of us. Nearly two years ago, he started sending me essays about his life, and the common denominator throughout each essay, whether on the surface or under the skin, was the idea of home- his particular home. Some of the stories took me right back to my childhood, to our common friends and experiences; however, many of the other stories revealed aspects of Jimi's life that I knew little about: living with cerebral palsy and learning disabilities; learning to drive through the help of a kind neighbor; being a caregiver for both of his parents in their dying days; finding the love of his life, Sherri; and finding God.

Even if I didn't know Jimi, the stories that make up this memoir ring true. They display honesty, humility, suffering, perseverance, and above all, humor. Lots of humor. Jimi has spent a lifetime helping others, whether it be as a Healthy Living Coach, as a Big Brother in the Big Brothers/Big Sisters of America organization, or as a loving son and a doting husband. He can now add inspiring and talented author to that list. Through reading his essays, he has invited me into his home yet again. You will be glad you took him up on his invitation as well.

Table of Contents

A Hook and a Limp with a Smile

The year was 1963. The Beatles released "I Want to Hold Your Hand". The song would rocket to number 1 on the charts as Beatlemania begins. John F. Kennedy was the President of the United States. In August of that year, Martin Luther King, Jr. delivers his "I Have a Dream" speech and I was born in Frankfurt Germany but, I'll get to that. The Andy Griffith Show was the most Popular TV Program. Jan and Dean's Surf City would become the song of the summer and my mom would give birth to me in the fall of that year. My name is Jimi Huckaby and this is my story. In many ways, I was a kid like most other kids that grew up in suburban America, except I was born with cerebral palsy effecting primarily my left side. While cerebral palsy (pronounced seh-ree-brel pawl-zee) is a blanket term commonly referred to as "CP" and described by a loss or impairment of motor function, cerebral palsy is actually caused by brain damage. The brain damage is caused by brain injury before birth, during birth, or immediately after birth. cerebral palsy primarily affects body movement and muscle coordination. Though cerebral palsy can be defined, having cerebral palsy does not define the person that has the condition.

These are my thoughts and feelings of growing up with cerebral palsy. I should start at the very beginning. My story begins on November 18th, 1963. At the time, my dad was a sergeant in the United States Army and was stationed in Frankfurt Germany. One afternoon, while he was out on maneuvers with his outfit, my mom was back at the apartment ironing. My oldest brother Biff had just come in from school and he had gone out to play. Suddenly the doorbell rang. When mom opened the door, she was shocked to see a G.I. standing there holding Biff who was completely covered with mud and blood. Biff was crying hysterically, and mom was concerned that he was hurt really bad. The guy said that Biff had been ran over by a German delivery truck. Of course, right away Biff had to be taken to the dispensary, so he could be seen by a doctor and have X-rays done.

My dad was notified immediately of the accident and he rushed back to be with mom. After a thorough examination, it was determined that Biff was "ok", except for some cuts and bruises. So, Biff was released, and they went home. Naturally, all this excitement really upset my mom. Then about 5:30, Mom started having pains. Since I wasn't due until January, she thought her body was just having a nervous reaction from the accident earlier in the day. When the pains kept up, she finally went back to the dispensary around 8:30. The doctor sent her to the Frankfurt Hospital by ambulance saying I could arrive at any moment. Well, with the help of Maj. Hoja, I did arrive at 10:28pm that night.

I have no way of knowing for sure, but I suspect that I was born with cerebral palsy because of the shock that my mom endured during the accident that occurred that day. I know I was very fortunate that my cerebral palsy wasn't any worse than it was. The bottom line is that it's irrelevant what caused it. Having cerebral palsy would prove to be very challenging. That doesn't necessarily mean it was a bad thing though.

Along with the CP, I also had something called lazy eye. Lazy eye is the eye condition noted by reduced vision not correctable by glasses. The brain, for some reason, does not fully acknowledge the images seen by the amblyopic eye. Back then, they would have me wear a patch over my good eye, as a way of strengthening the bad eye. I was also cross eyed. When I was 5 years old, I had surgery on my right eye to correct that problem.

As a child, I have no memory of ever hearing the definition of cerebral palsy and my parents never explained it to me. Because of the time, I'm not sure they themselves knew much about it. One thing was very clear to me, I sure knew I wasn't like the other kids. I had to wear a brace on my left leg that went down my leg and attached to my shoe. My left foot turned inward, and the brace was to force it not to do that. As a small child with a bad limp, it didn't take long for me to realize that I was different. Because I would drag my left foot while walking, I would often fall. My left arm and hand were also affected by the cerebral palsy. Often my left arm was drawn up close to my body and that hand would turn under making the shape of a hook. Looking back, I think if you were born with a disability in the 1960's you had to grow up a little faster than other kids. I learned from a very early age that if you were physically different in anyway there was going to be hell to pay for it. In other words, if you were different, you were going to be teased, picked on and bullied. That is just the way it was. Elementary school was very tough. During the seventh grade, the endless bullying reached its peak. Thankfully, early that year I befriended a boy named Chet Steelman. Well, Chet had been in special ed classes because he was a little slow and had recently been put into regular classes. He and I had home room together. While in the seventh grade Chet was about 15 years old. That meant he was considerably bigger than all the other guys in class. After I befriended Chet, if anyone picked on me then Chet would just beat the crap out of them. I was the smallest kid in class and Chet was by far the biggest. He always protected me. I think it was kind of like watching a bulldog protecting a mouse. On the days when he wasn't there, the bullying would be particularly bad. Because of having CP, I also had a learning disability. Because of that, I was poor in Math and English. I grew to hate school. It bothered my mom so much to see me struggling at school, that there were times that she literally did my homework for me. She knew how hard I was trying just to keep from failing. Because of my poor reading skills, on the days that I had an oral book report, I would actually become sick to my stomach. The only subject I enjoyed in school was Art. I loved to draw. I also loved music, small animals and summertime, because if it was summer, I wasn't in school.

At home things were much better for two reasons. Number 1, the kids in my neighborhood didn't pick on me. Number 2, my parents didn't treat me like I had a disability. In other words, I had the same chores as my siblings like taking out the trash, mowing the yard, cleaning my room etc. That became an invaluable part of my upbringing, because it taught me that I really could do the same things that my other abled bodied siblings could do. I wasn't given a pass just because I had cerebral palsy. I was expected to pull my own weight.

As a teenager, finding someone to date was a rarity. Young people are very superficial. For some reason, girls just didn't find a really skinny guy with a bad arm and a limp to be sexy. :-)

To make things a little more complicated and challenging, my dad was always telling me I "couldn't do this" or I "couldn't do that". He told me I "couldn't" learn to drive a car. Thankfully, a neighbor across the street, (Roger Phelps) volunteered to teach me how to drive. For my dad the fact that I learned how to drive turned out to be a real blessing because after he suffered a stroke, I was the one that took him to his doctor appointments.

For most of my life I have used humor to deal with my cerebral palsy. I refer to my crippled arm as "the hook". It's common for my crippled hand to drop things because if I open my right hand then my left hand opens simultaneously. This is called "modeling". The same is true if I turn my hand a certain angle, then involuntarily my crippled hand will turn the same angle. These kinds of things can cause some rather humorous things to occur. Once, while I was standing in line behind my friend Greg getting pizza at a Mr. Gatti's buffet, one of these silly, unexplainable incidents occurred. Each time I would scoop a piece of pizza up with the spatula and turn my wrist to put it on my plate, my crippled hand would turn the plate downward causing my pizza to fall on the floor. No matter how careful I tried to be, each time my pizza ended up one the floor. By the time my third piece of pizza had hit the floor, an older lady behind me blurted out, "Are you going to drop all of this pizza on the floor?!" I laughed and said "sorry". At that point, Greg noticed the pizza on the floor, and he knew what had happened and busted out laughing. Greg wasn't laughing at me. He was laughing at the situation. Greg knew how limited my hands were to the point that he would always carry my drink to the table for me. He knew I couldn't carry a plate of food and a drink at the same time. To show my twisted sense of humor, I use to joke that I was going to get a job as a waiter. There would be broken glass all over the floor in the restaurant because of my inability to carry the plates the glasses to the tables.

As you can see, having a disability isn't all bad. It can make you stronger. Because of my disability, I became very determined. As a young adult, I wanted to get a job like my siblings and my friends had done, but my dad was strongly opposed to the idea because he was afraid I would lose my disability benefits and then be unable to financially take care of myself. He and I would have fierce arguments about my strong desire to get a job. In his defense, he obviously knew he would die some day and wouldn't be here to take care of me. He felt that as long as I was on social security disability then I would be taken care of. I pushed so hard to get a job because I wanted to take care of myself. I wanted to feel like I was contributing something to society. Having a job made me feel valued. It gave me self-worth and it gave me independence. Working was very important to me. My dad taught all of us kids to work hard and to earn an honest wage. I wanted to prove to him and myself that I could do it. I didn't stand up to my dad very often, but this was one battle worth having and I wasn't going to back down. Against his wishes, I finally got a job at the Bullitt County YMCA. I was hired to clean the whirlpools and to be the evening and weekend janitor. I would learn that because of my disability I would have to do things differently than most of the workers there, but I would usually figure a way to get things done. I would later become the first Wellness Center Attendant that the Bullitt County YMCA ever had. I would set members up on an exercise workout routine. I've now worked there for more than 25 years. That's not bad for an old crippled man. Ha!

I would later be diagnosed with an eye disease called Fuchs Dystrophy. The disease can greatly affect your vision. It would take two corneal transplants to improve my vision. A short time after that I would sustain a bulging disc in my back and that would greatly impact my active lifestyle. These recent health concerns would prove to be very challenging. Oddly enough, I firmly believe if I hadn't already dealt with having cerebral palsy, it would have been far more difficult to handle my more recent health issues. It proves that over all having cerebral palsy has been a blessing. There is a lot to be said for faith, willpower and determination.

These days, my wife (Sherri) and I have a three-legged cat named Tom. I limp and so does Tom. I've told Sherri that now she has two of us limping around the house. I find it somewhat ironic and humorous that a crippled man would end up with a crippled cat. Well crippled and all, I think Tom and I are enjoying a pretty amazing journey just limping through this life. God is good. :-)

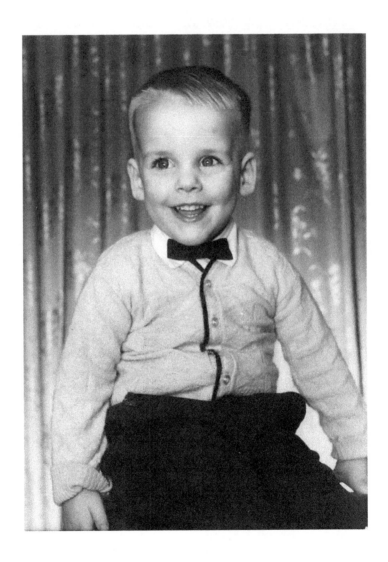

Mom & Daddy and Our New Home

It was 1967, The Beatles released "Sgt. Pepper's Lonely Hearts Club Band" album to critical acclaim. Lyndon B. Johnson was our nations President and the Vietnam War raged on. Elvis Presley and Priscilla Beaulieu were married in Las Vegas. On June 16th, The Monterey Pop Music Festival begins and is held for 3 days. It was the summer of love and my family moved into our new home on 1503 Riverview Drive in Shepherdsville, Kentucky. At the time, I was only 3 years old. It has now been more then 50 years that I have lived in the same house. This book is a group of thoughts and memories I have of growing up in my house on Riverview Drive in Shepherdsville Kentucky.

More than a half a century ago, when my parents brought our home, the house number was 1503 Riverview Drive. About 25 years later the house number and street name were changed. The street name was changed from Riverview Drive to Riverview Lane.

Shortly after moving into our home, my dad got a job at General Electric and settled in to living his new life as a civilian. Even though my dad had retired from the Army he would forever remain a soldier at heart. My dad was hard, disciplined and very strict, but he was a good, hardworking man. All 4 of us kids are hard workers because he taught us to work hard. Dad was from Wartburg Tennessee and my Mom was from Clermont Kentucky. They both grew up dirt poor in southern rural America. In the south you were raised to address your parents as Momma and Daddy. That is how I addressed them until I was nearly grown. Then I began calling my mother Mom but, I continued to call my father Daddy for the rest of his life. When it came to Mom, my dad lead by example on how to treat a lady. It was common for my dad to come and kiss Mom when he would go somewhere without her. She would never say goodbye. She would always say, "be careful" as he went out the door. I think Mom rarely said goodbye to anyone. Dad loved to eat apples. After cutting an apple into 4 pieces he would always go and give Mom 2 pieces of it. Even years later after my dad had a stroke, he still never forgot Mom's birthday or Valentine's Day. She was the love of his life and it showed.

I grew up during a time when people stayed together, and divorce wasn't as common as it is today. I only had 2 friends whose parents divorced. I was very fortunate. I had wonderful parents. No one is perfect and they had their flaws, but I know I was very fortunate to be raised by the parents I had. They both exemplified honesty and integrity. They were simple people. My parents were a cross between Archie and Edith Bunker of "All in The Family" and Jack and Norma Arnold from "The Wonder Years". My dad was a huge supporter of union rights and my mom was a strong supporter of women's rights. My parents were 100% Democrat and very proud of it because they both felt like the Democratic Party did more for hard working, middle class people. My parents taught us kids to have strong opinions and beliefs and to stand by them.

While living in Germany, my mom became very sick with pneumonia. It was so bad one of her lungs collapsed and she nearly died. My dad was so afraid of losing her that, he would insist that anytime Mom would get sick, that she go see a doctor immediately. He was very protective of her.

One of the differences in Mom and Dad was that my dad loved to sit on the front porch. He liked for Mom to sit out there with him. She would sit out there with him often, but Mom enjoyed sitting in the back yard more. She would always say that Dad liked sitting on the porch because he was so nosey; he was afraid he might miss something going on in the neighborhood. Mom liked the privacy and the quiet of the back yard. Mom used to tell me that I was just like my dad. I never took that as a compliment and I never really believed it either. Ha! My oldest brother Biff use to tell me that I have far more patience than anyone else in the family. I don't really feel very patient sometimes. My dad had no patience at all. He always wanted everything done right away. I think I more than likely developed patience from dealing with my handicap. Generally, I tend to be slower paced then he was, and I take much longer to get things done.

I give things a great deal of thought before I do them. Dad liked for things to be taken care of ahead of time and he hated to be late. I'm very much like that as well. My dad was a huge Tennessee Volunteers football fan and I too became a big UT fan. The fact that I look like my dad is absolutely, undeniable. Gee, thanks Dad.

I do have a lot of my mom's characteristics and interests as well. Mom was a night owl and so am I. She had a love for antique shops and so do I. My Mom enjoyed writing and I have developed that as well. My mom's liberal views are the reason that I am comfortable worshipping in a church that's open to blacks and whites. We both loved Louisville Cardinal basketball and Christmas time. Like my Mother, I too like my privacy and I myself enjoy sitting in the back yard more than the front porch as well. As a result, I know far less about what goes on in the neighborhood then my dad ever did simply because I'm not nosey enough to find out. Ha! I am proudly a product of both of my parents. I guess, I should be proud of who I came from. The older I get, the more like them I become.

Jimi age 4

Early Memories on Riverview Drive

My memories of growing up in the suburbs during the 1970's are endless. There were lots of sights and sounds of growing up in the suburbs back then. The sound of a lawnmower and the smell of freshly mowed lawn. The laughter of kids playing hide and seek. The sound of the ice cream truck coming from off in the distance. The smell of a neighbor grilling out on a warm summer evening.

Why wouldn't I have a special fondness for summertime as a kid? I mean, we moved into my childhood home during the summer. I truly feel very blessed to have had the wonderful childhood that I had. It's a rather simple story. My dad had just recently retired from the Army after 24 years and he had moved his family to Kentucky. I was the youngest of 4 kids. At the time I was nearly 4 years old and it was the summer of 1967 when my parents moved me, my two brothers and sister into our new home on Riverview Drive. My early memories of living on Riverview Dr. mostly involve the dog days of summer and the new friends I made in the neighborhood. My brother Jerry and I became friends with Denise Phelps and Tony Morgan from across the street. We would all pile in Tony's mom's station wagon and go to the Preston Drive-in to see an old Disney movie or a Charlie Brown movie. I remember seeing The Love Bug, Bedknobs and Broomsticks and The Jungle Book. Sometimes on a hot summer day Tony's mom would take us to L&N Golf Club to go swimming. That was always lots of fun.

Back then, our next-door neighbor had an old brown and white basset hound named Missy. Well, on a stifling hot summer afternoon, Missy would sonder out into the middle of Riverview Drive and she would lay down and go to sleep. Eventually, a car would come over the hill and stop and wait until Missy would finally get up and slowly move out of the road.

My mom and dad had quickly become good friends with Denise's parents (Roger & Doris Phelps). On warm summer evenings they would walk over and sit on the porch and talk to my parents while Jerry and I would run around the yard catching lighting bugs. At dusk, I also enjoyed catching frogs at the end of Tony's driveway under the streetlight. Ahhhhh, to be a little boy again. The sweet innocence of childhood is too often taken for granted.

In those days, there was also all the excitement in the neighborhood that was brought around by the sound of the ice cream man. Kids would hear the music from the ice cream truck coming from a mile away. Then, they would run home as fast as they could to get money for ice cream. The many ice cream options were endless. You could pick a Crunch Bar, a Creamsicle, an Ice Cream Sandwich, a Fudgesicle or my personal favorite, the Drumstick. The Drumstick was a crunchy waffle cone that was stuffed full of creamy vanilla ice cream. On top of the Drumstick cone was a hard shell of chocolate covered in nuts. At the bottom of the waffle cone you were pleasantly surprised to find a chunk of milk chocolate waiting for you. Yummy, now those were the days!

Those wonderful summers seemed to last a lifetime back then and they were full of fun and laughter. Yes, those were my earliest memories of my life on Riverview Drive.

Patti Sue, Jimi, Biff & Jerry

From Patti Sue to Patricia

I have one sister and two brothers. My sister is the oldest. These are my thoughts and memories of my big sister. Her name is Patricia. When I was little, we called her Patti Sue. It wasn't until many years later that I started calling her Patricia. I was born with cerebral palsy affecting my left side. When I was little, I wore a brace on my left leg. Once before church, I remember my sister Patti Sue being responsible for getting this leg brace on me. Well, I wouldn't sit still, and I didn't like the brace so getting it on me could be a little bit of a challenge. There was a small wire that stuck out of the side of the brace. Years later, Patti Sue told me that it ruined a few pairs of her pantyhose. Once while Mom and Dad were gone, Patti Sue was in charge of watching us kids, I misbehaved, and she corrected me. Then, I got mad and cussed at her. She warned me if I said that again she would wash my mouth out with soap. With a dare like that, I just couldn't resist and so I said it again. BIG MISTAKE! The next thing I know, Patti had me in a headlock and drug me to the bathroom and she stuffed a wet bar of soap in my mouth. Needless-to-say, she cleaned up my vocabulary. YUCK!

Most of my memories of my big sister are good ones. When I was a small child, I remember Patti Sue, Jerry and I lying in bed together singing Christmas carols out of a song book. I still have that song book. That is a warm holiday memory. On another occasion, Patti Sue took Jerry and I to see the movie Scrooge. That was fun. Patti Sue liked to sew. I remember she would sit in the floor and cut out dress patterns and make some of her own clothes. As a teenager, I also remember Patti having several friends come to the house. Teresa, Poogie and Mark just to name a few. I vaguely remember them sitting around the kitchen table playing a board game, while watching the Winter Olympics.

My sister is 10 years older than me. That doesn't sound like much nowadays, but when I was a kid it seemed like a much bigger gap. That meant when I was 10 years old, she was 20 and possibly already out of the house. Basically, after that I didn't see her as much. She married Roger Patterson and then Roger was drafted into the Army. Shortly thereafter, they were moved to Frankfurt Germany. Patti Sue would send letters to Jerry and I from Germany. I remember she sent Jerry and I both an advent calendar at Christmas time. I still have mine and I have one of those letters she sent as well.

Just a few short years later Patti Sue and Roger moved back to the United States. For a short time, they lived in the basement and it was great having them home. I remember Patti taking me and my friend Archie to see the first Star Wars movie. That is still my favorite Star Wars movie.

Patti Sue and Roger bought a trailer and moved it to a holler off of Bells Mill Road. Jerry and I loved to go spend the weekend with Patti Sue and Roger. We would have a blast! Down the hill from the trailer they lived in was a creek. We would spend hours swimming and wading in that creek and then sometimes Patti Sue would make us her trademark homemade lasagna. It was delicious. Or sometimes, Roger would make us his five- alarm chili and it was yummy too. Sometimes after dark we would walk down the hill to Ma's house. There were no streetlights anywhere close by. It was so dark outside you literally couldn't see your hand in front of your face. Patti Sue would make us join hands and then she would lead us down the hill. When late night came, we'd watch Saturday Night Live, then we would go to sleep on a big white long-haired rug that lay on the floor in the living room. After I got a little older and got into music, I remember Patti Sue giving me her "Pink Floyd, The Wall" album. I thought that was very cool. I still have it.

Then things got even better. Patti Sue and Roger had their son Roger Demian Patterson. It was after Patti Sue had Demian that I started calling her Patricia. Roger and Patricia gave our parents their first and only Grandson and oh what a wonderful gift that was! That little guy was something very special. During this time, Roger had been going to Rets Electronic School. After he finished school, he took a job somewhere in

Indiana. He would commute back and forth. Patricia moved back home and then, she enrolled in Elizabethtown Community College to become a nurse. That is when Patricia gave me a truly wonderful gift. She asked me if I would babysit Demian while she was going to school. I wasn't crazy about the idea. I enjoyed my freedom to run around and do what I wanted but, I knew she was in a tight spot, so I agreed to do it. Looking back, it was a great decision. As it turned out, I would never father any kids of my own. Those couple of years I had helping out with Demian were the closet I would ever come to raising a child. I have my big sister to thank for that. In doing that, she gave me a wonderful gift. Demian was as perfect a child as anyone could ever hope for. He was about 3 or 4 when I first started keeping him. He was very well behaved and easily entertained. He would sit and watch TV or quietly read a comic book for hours. Demian loved The Muppet Show. He had the toy Animal puppet from The Muppet Show. He carried his Animal puppet everywhere and played with it all the time until he finally wore it out. Demian also really enjoyed Sesame Street. If I was in the kitchen when Sesame Street came on, he would insist that I come in there with him to help him sing the opening theme song. In the evening he would watch "The Dukes of Hazzard" with Papa. That is what he called his grandpa. At night, when Papa would go to bed, Demian would follow him in the bedroom then Papa would give him one stick of gum. Demian would come and offer a small piece of gum to everyone else in the house. Depending on how many were home sometimes he would tear his stick of gum into 4 or 5 pieces to share with everyone. In the fall I would always rake leaves. I would fill the wheelbarrow up with leaves and then sit Demian on top of the leaves. Then I would run through the yard pushing Demian as he sat atop a mountain of leaves. He would be giggling and laughing the whole time. Those days were full of fun and innocence. Those are truly some of my favorite memories and I have my big sister to thank for that. Playing an important role in my nephew's life when he was so small was an honor. He was very special to me.

Roger, Patricia and Demian would soon move away and make a new life for themselves. My parents and I would miss them terribly. The house seemed so quiet and empty for a while after that, but life moves on and so did I. Roger and Patricia would go on to have a daughter. Her name is Deidre. By that point, they lived away from us and I wasn't able to get as close to Deidre as I was to Demian. Even with Demian, I would learn that distance changes everything when dealing with a child. We would continue to get together a couple of times a year and always on Christmas. My big sister would go on to have grandchildren of her own and I'm sure she is an awesome grandma but, they better behave. Take it from someone who knows, if those grandkids give her any lip, she sure won't hesitate to wash their mouth out with soap, that is for sure!

Looking back, I know I've been very blessed to have had the sister I have. My sister has always been a "yes you can" person and that is awesome. She played a big role in making my childhood as rich as it was. As an adult, I enjoy visiting her whenever possible and I always enjoy our political conversations. Life keeps us both busy and we don't talk as often as we should but, I love her and I'm proud to have her as my big sister.

Daddy and her sister on the day she graduated from nursing school.

Biff (Brothers and Friends)

Biff is........ Confident, bold, strong willed, opinionated, loyal and very generous. Biff is also my oldest brother. He is six years older than I am. I also have one other brother, (Jerry) and a sister, (Patricia) When we first moved to Kentucky, we lived with my Aunt Rose and Uncle Dukie until Mom and Dad found a house. Patricia was 14, Biff was 10, Jerry was 5 and I was 4 when we moved into our new home on Riverview Drive. In the beginning Biff, Jerry and I had to share a bedroom together. Patricia had her own room. After Patricia moved out then Biff got her bedroom. Biff played a major role in what would later become my passion for music. As a teenager, he joined a book and record club. I think it may have been Columbia House but I'm not sure. He would order cassette tapes and sometimes he would let Jerry and I pick out something for ourselves as well. That is when I first heard the country comedian Jerry Clower. Biff bought me the Jerry Clower cassettes "Country Ham" and "Clower Power". I listened to them so much I wore them out. A few summers ago, I bought them on record at a flea market because you can't get them on CD. Back then Biff also bought Jerry something too. Fittingly enough, he got Jerry the Cal Smith cassette "Country Bumpkin" and a Tom T. Hall cassette.

Biff enjoyed sports. He liked the Kentucky Colonels, the Dallas Cowboys, the Tennessee Volunteers and the Louisville Cardinals. By today's standards Biff would have been a child that clearly had hyperactivity disorder. He was very high energy and always on the move. He was the athletic one in the family. He was always playing a pickup basketball, football or baseball game in the neighborhood. Biff was repeatedly getting hurt. Weather it was just some bumps, bruises, scrapes or dislocated bones. He could even come up with a surprise injury from partially falling through the roof over our basement entrance. A fall which required several stitches. At the time, he was just trying to get a frisbee off the roof.

Oddly enough for someone that was so active, Biff also really enjoyed reading. He read a lot of books. As a teenager, he also enjoyed cooking. He enjoyed baking. He would make no bake cookies. They were very good. Daddy called them "cow piles". He loved them and so did I.

Biff got his first job at Key Market in Shepherdsville then he and Patricia both worked at the Holiday House restaurant. Biff then bought a 1965 mustang. He drove the car fast and with reckless abandon. Predictably enough, shortly thereafter he blew the motor up in the car. A neighbor on our street (Bernard Hardwick) put another motor in the car for him and Biff was on the go again.

Once, he came home from work with a gift that he bought for me. It was an album by the bubblegum group The Ohio Express. The album had the hits "Yummy, Yummy, Yummy" and "Chewy, Chewy" on it. Bubblegum music was happy, upbeat music. It was very corny music but as a kid, I loved it. To this day, I still listen to some of those corny songs on my iPod. During the Christmas holiday season, he got me a silly Christmas album by a group called The Caroleers. I loved that one as well. When I was very little, I remember WKLO radio playing daily in our house. Also, my sister Patricia and Biff had a collection of records that I would listen to whenever I had the chance. They had the old 45 records of "Nice To Be With You" by Gallery, "Elusive Butterfly" by Bob Lind, "Abraham, Martin And John" by Dion, "Atlantis" by Donavon, "A Hard Day's Night" and "Please, Please Me" by The Beatles, "I'm A Believer" and "Pleasant Valley Sunday" both by The Monkees, just to name a few. I wore those records out. Biff had the cassette "Hot August Night" by Neil Diamond. When Biff was gone, I would go into his bedroom and turn his stereo up and listen to that cassette. That album was electric, a pure masterpiece! It would go on to become the best work of Neil Diamond's career.

I grew older, Biff moved out and married his girlfriend Anita. As it turned out, the marriage didn't last, and Biff moved out west to Oklahoma for work. I didn't see him as much for a while. He started dating a girl named

Sondra and they would make trips back and forth to visit. Mom and Daddy took a trip out there to see them with Aunt Rose and Doyle. For a short time, Biff and Sondra moved to Somerset Kentucky and it was at that time that we would all make trips to Gatlinburg in the Great Smoky Mountains of Tennessee. Those are some priceless memories. Taking those trips with our parents to Gatlinburg, especially at Christmas time was great fun. Just walking the sidewalks of Gatlinburg with Mom, Daddy, Biff and Sondra while enjoying the simple things. Daddy was always planning our next meal. Those were wonderful times. It was during this time that Biff and I would get close. He and Sondra would later get married in a wedding chapel in Gatlinburg. I was honored to be his best man.

Again, Biff and Sondra moved back out west. Then they had a daughter and named her Cami. It was a special time and she brought a lot of joy. Mom and Daddy were very excited to have a new grandchild. For her first Christmas, Daddy bought Cami a stuffed rappin' Santa at Big Lots. Biff learned how to make Mom's fudge. Now at Christmas time, Biff makes Mom's peanut butter fudge and passes it out to family and friends just like she did. Biff also does most of the cooking for his own family. He is a good cook.

Biff and Sondra would go on to have another daughter. Her name is Kaycee. She was born with a head full of thick hair and Mom and Daddy were crazy about her.

Given the fact of what strong Democrats our parents were, it's shocking that any of my siblings would become anything but a Democrat. Daddy was an Army veteran and a blue-collar worker that believed strongly in unions. Mom was a strong supporter of women's rights. Both of our parents were big Democrats until the day they died. Biff somehow turned out to be the only Republican my parents ever had. Given the fact of how progressive our parents were, it's downright comical that their oldest son would grow up to become a Republican. Once, Biff even had his picture taken with George W. Bush. He even told George W. that Mom would be rolling over in her grave because he did that. Ha!

As the years went by, Biff and I lost both of our parents, I would marry a lady with a beautiful soul named Sherri. Biff would lose Sondra after a long hard battle with breast cancer. He would go on and find love again in a lady from Kansas named Bobbi. She seems like a wonderful person and Biff seems happy again.

Throughout my life, Biff has been there through the good times and bad. He is a man of great integrity. He is a lead by example kind of guy. Biff is a pillar of strength and I'm proud to have him as a brother. I love him as a brother, and we are also friends. That's a pretty special thing.

Jerry (The Quiet One)

Jerry is ....Very unique, he is country, witty, quiet, a hard worker and loyal. Jerry is a lot of things. But most importantly to me, Jerry is my brother. He is a middle child and the closest to me in age. I have one other brother and a sister. I'm the youngest of us four kids. When we first moved into our house on Riverview Drive, Biff, Jerry and I all shared a bedroom together and Patti Sue had her own bedroom. At that time, Jerry and I slept on bunk beds. Jerry slept on the top bunk and I slept on the bottom. Biff had a twin bed. Whenever I was very little, Jerry and I were close. I idealized him. I followed Jerry everywhere and for some unknown reason I called him "Serge" That was short for Sergeant. My Dad was a Sergeant in the Army. I'm sure that's where I got the idea to call Jerry, "Serge". When my sister moved out, Biff got her room and Jerry and I shared a room together. Jerry and I enjoyed getting up on Sunday mornings to watch Abbott and Costello and staying up late to watch old Marx Brothers films. For some reason, we both also enjoyed sitting out on the front porch while listening to Daddy talk to Mr. Phelps. We enjoyed listening to them tell old stories or just talk about the events of the day. We also enjoyed going to my sister's trailer on the weekends and hanging out with her. Back then, we did quite a bit together. We had a few of the same friends. Tony Morgan, Denise Phelps, CW Spurlock, Chris Logan, Shannon Weaver and later Mike White. At different times, we'd run around at the old graveyard, play games, ride bikes or camp out. Jerry's first girlfriend was the girl next door. Her name was Regina Spurlock. She was a babe. I remember thinking, "Wow, he is lucky!" Believe it or not, Regina was a prettier version of Winnie on "The Wonder Years".

When we were kids, Jerry took up oil painting. I remember him painting an old locomotive in one of his paintings and a log cabin in another. Jerry and I were both artistic in our own way. For a short time, Jerry took up guitar lessons, but he didn't stick to it.

Time has a way of changing things. By our teenage years we had clearly grown apart. Like all brothers do, we'd fight because we wanted our own space. We had grown sick of sharing a room together. We got on each other's nerves. By this time, we had completely different friends and we liked entirely different things. I liked hard rock and Jerry liked bluegrass. I listened to bands like The Who and Jerry listened to Bill Monroe and The Blue Grass Boys. I liked sports and Jerry was into things like the Future Farmers of America. Jerry was always drawn to country things. When he was a teenager, he bought himself an old army jeep and he would go off- roading. I was into rock concerts and Jerry was into tractor pulls. We were just very different.

After a failed attempt of joining the Army, Jerry went away to a school in Nashville and became a diesel mechanic. He came home and got a job at Diesel Injection Service and shortly thereafter he married Diana. She had a daughter named Chantel from a previous marriage. Jerry adopted Chantel. She was a great kid that grew into an outstanding young lady. After 20 something years of marriage Jerry shocked the family by announcing that he and Diana were getting a divorce. This all happened during the last days of my mom's life. Mom had been battling dementia for a few years and I had been taking care of her. By this point, Jerry had stepped up his game and was helping me out more taking care of Mom. A couple of times I had called Jerry in the middle of the night to help me with her and without hesitation he came right over. I guess, in a crisis you either get closer or you pull apart. Thankfully, Jerry and I got closer.

Jerry would later marry Denise. She is very nice, and Jerry seems happy. Their house has Jerry's country character all over it. Sherri and I have them over for cookout's every summer and we go to their house for Thanksgiving dinner. Jerry still comes over to help me seal the driveway every 2 years. I don't call on Jerry often but anytime I do he is always there. Jerry has always had a quiet confidence. Like the rest of us kids, he's very opinionated. He has my mom's love of antique's and her country style and my Dad's hard work ethic and he holds both of our parent's strong political views. He's an unapologetic Democrat through and through. Jerry also reminds me a lot of my Uncle Carl. Mom used to say the same thing. Jerry even walks like Uncle Carl. My Uncle Carl is a great guy so that is a compliment.

Because Jerry is so quiet, I have no idea what he thinks of me. But I know what I think of him. I'm proud to have Jerry as my brother. If I were ever in a war, I would want Jerry in the foxhole right next to me. I believe he would be fighting until we both got out of there. That's a pretty awesome thing.

Going to Granny's

When I was little, once a year we would go on vacation. If that's what you called it. Our vacations always consisted of going to see my Granny and my Aunt Wilma and Uncle Harry. Granny was my dad's mom and my Aunt Wilma was my dad's sister. They lived next door to each other on Hays Street in Rossville Georgia. My Uncle Ross (My Dad's brother) and my Aunt Rema (My Dad's other sister) lived with my Granny. It was a joy to go visit them all. My dachshund would always make the trip with us. Hootie was her name and I got her on my first birthday. Hootie would always get excited the night before the big trip, as soon as my Mom would get out the suitcases. Our long trip to get there would always start before daylight. My dad would get us all up at about 4:30 in the morning. We would stuff the backseat with pillows, blankets, books and a small tape player. I remember listening to a cassette of Jerry Clower, that my brother Biff got me. Jerry Clower was a country comedian that told funny stories. I loved hearing those old stories. My brother Jerry had the cassettes of Cal Smith singing Country Bumpkin and Tom T. Hall singing "Old Dogs, Children and Watermelon Wine". Those are two of my favorite country songs of all time, partly because of listening to them on those long trips. We would listen to our music while, we prompted the big trucks to honk their horns for us. That was always fun. Miles and hours down the road, we would finally get to stop at a Stuckey's. We would get some greasy burgers and Jerry and I would get some Mexican jumping beans or maybe some cheap toy like a slingshot.

After what seemed like 12 hours on the road, we would finally reach Granny's house in only about 6 hours. Stuffing 3 or 4 kids, in the back seat of a car can certainly make for a long road trip. We were always happy to finally get there. Granny's house had a wooden screen door and I remember it would squeak whenever you opened it and slam when you shut it. That sound became synonymous with being at Granny's house. We would always go in and sit down and visit with Granny first, before going next door to see Aunt Wilma and Uncle Harry. I always enjoyed hearing Granny talk. I can't put my finger on it, but she always made me smile. It was clear that Granny didn't have much money and she couldn't afford to buy us kids anything, but that didn't mean a thing to me. Granny was a special lady and just being around her was a treat. Aunt Rema would come out and visit with us too. She was a very religious, soft spoken lady, that spoke with a slow southern drawl. Sometimes Uncle Ross would be gone somewhere working. Uncle Ross walked everywhere because he didn't have a car. Sometimes, he would give Jerry and I some kind of odd gift. I think it would be a pocketknife or something else that he had found while walking all over town. We would always take whatever kind of interesting thing it was and say thank you.

Then we would all go next door to visit Aunt Wilma and Uncle Harry. Aunt Wilma would spoil us when we came to visit. She would always have Brown Cow ice cream bars and ice cream sandwiches for us. Aunt Wilma was a wonderful cook and she would always have a cake baked as well, usually a coconut cake or a German chocolate cake. Even though Aunt Wilma didn't seem like an animal person, she had a bulldog for years. Dad and Aunt Wilma were very close. I'm sure it was because they were a lot alike. Biff was Aunt Wilma's favorite of us kids and she made that pretty obvious. She called him Biffy. Sometimes he would spend the whole summer with them. They would shower all of us kids with lots of fun gifts and plenty of love.

After we visited with Aunt Wilma, we would walk through the gate back over to Granny's house. Granny didn't have air conditioning, so in the late afternoon she would sit on her back porch, because it was too hot to stay in the house. She had big walnut trees in her back yard. While Granny would sit there swatting flies with her ever present fly swatter, we would crack walnuts that had fallen off of those trees. After dark we would go in and watch a little TV before bed. On occasion, you may really be interested in watching a show and all at once, Granny would notice that it was her bedtime and she would just get up and turn the TV off and then start turning all the lights out and go to bed. My brother Jerry and I would sleep in Granny's feather bed. It would be kind of a treat. After a long and busy day, I would lay there in the silence waiting to drift off to sleep and I would hear Granny's clock coo cooing from the living room. Just like the slamming of Granny's screen door, the sound of that coo coo clock became synonymous with a visit to Granny's house. Warm and wonderful memories from time long gone by now. Gone but never forgotten.

The next morning Aunt Wilma would fix a hardy, southern style breakfast complete with homemade biscuits, jelly, gravy, sausage, fried potatoes and eggs. It was always yummy. After that we may either head off to Gatlinburg Tennessee or we would start back home. If we went to Gatlinburg, we would spend a day or two shopping and go to the Ripley's believe it or not museum. We would have to sneak Hootie into the hotel room, because back then hotels didn't allow animals. Jerry and I would always run down to get ice from the ice maker and checkout the vending machines. The whole family would walk around Gatlinburg until after dark and then retire to the hotel room. Jerry and I would play with the magic fingers thing on the bed by putting a quarter in it. Magic fingers is something that made the bed vibrate. I'm sure it was something to use while having sex but at the time Jerry and I knew nothing about that, we would just turn it on for fun. Once while staying in Gatlinburg Mom paid for us to watch the movie "The Towering Inferno" on our hotel TV. We stayed up late watching it. That was fun. The next morning, we would eat breakfast and head back to our house on Riverview Dr.

Looking back, I think the simplest memories are the best memories and in visiting my Granny, there were plenty of
simple memories. She led a simple life and because I was just a child, things were much more simple for me as well. My Granny made me smile and when you're a kid, that's a pretty wonderful thing.

My Granny (Mary Huckaby)

Four generations. Patricia, Demian, Granny and Daddy

CW's Fishing Trip Run Amuck

After we had lived in our house for a while the Spurlock family moved in next door. The Spurlock's had 2 kids, a boy and a girl, C.W. and Regina. Jerry and I became friends with C.W. and Regina. Occasionally, our parents would get together with Mr. and Mrs. Spurlock and play rook until 1 or 2 in the morning. Jerry and I enjoyed it because that meant we could get together and hangout with C.W. and Regina and play broad games or cards. By today's standards C.W. would have been a kid that clearly had attention deficit and hyperactivity disorder. C.W. was very high energy and silly if not just downright goofy. He laughed a lot and would sometimes get so tickled that he would pee in his pants. C.W. was always in trouble. There are a few stories about C.W. that are legendary. With that being said, this story comes to mind.

One time, C.W.'s dad had purchased an expensive rod and reel, because he had planned to take the family fishing while on vacation. He gave C.W. strict orders not to touch it while he was at work. Well, C.W. just couldn't resist. Shortly after his dad left for work, C.W. got that rod and reel and ran out into the back yard with it. At the end of the fishing line, on this nice fishing pole, was a huge sinker. C.W. was so excited because he was going to cast this rod and reel for the first time. With no hesitation he pulled back on the pole, and with one hard motion he cast that sinker high into the air, but it quickly wrapped itself around a power line about 15 feet off the ground. Well, after getting some bad advice on what to do next from the rest of us kids standing around, C.W. proceeded to wind the reel on the rod until the fishing pole was so high off the ground that you had to reach up to even touch it. Then attempting to unwind the fishing line from the wire he slung it as hard as he could over the power line. All at once the fishing line broke and the fishing pole came crashing to the ground, breaking the reel on the rod. When Mr. Spurlock got home C.W. got a spanking and was grounded AGAIN. When I think back on what happened that day, I think it was like an episode of Leave It To Beaver, but from the

1970's. Only this stuff really happened! Thank you C.W. for giving me this wonderful childhood memory to share over 40 years later. Childhood friends forever remain friends because it's a moment in time and in our memories they live forever.

Another Fine Mess

This is a story about a great friend I had while growing up. His name is Chris Logan. I was a few years older than Chris. The first time he and I met we played with his Johnny West action figures on his front porch. Chris had the biggest imagination of any kid I ever knew. When I first met Chris, he was little. He would make his own paper dolls and play with them, but they weren't the kind of paper dolls that little girls play with. He would draw things like Batman & Robin, the Joker, Superman, Spider-Man, The Three Stooges and many more. He would cut them out and play with them. Like I said, Chris had a wide-open imagination. Chris and I both enjoyed old comedy teams like Abbott & Costello, Laurel & Hardy and The Three Stooges. My personal favorite was the Marx Brothers. When we were little we would get together and pretend to be Laurel & Hardy. Chris was always Laurel and I was Hardy. If my brother Jerry was with us, we would all pretend to be The Three Stooges. Jerry would be Moe, I would be Larry and Chris would be Curly. Then we would slap, pinch, knock and punch each other silly the rest of the afternoon.

Once his parents took us to see the Apple Dumpling Gang and we came home, went out in the yard and pretended to be those silly characters from the movie. Chris enjoyed old shows like The Six Million Dollar Man, Batman and Starsky & Hutch. He and I used to just sit in his mom's car and pretend to be Starsky & Hutch. On occasion Chris and I would take an old GI Joe or some other unfortunate action figure and slide it down the road back and forth to each other until there would be nothing left of it. Once when Chris's parents were having their driveway concreted the two of us threw a couple of action figures down right before the concrete was poured just so we could watch them being buried in concrete. Yes, I know that is strange but, this is the kind of silly things that boys do until they discover girls.

Something else that Chris and I enjoyed together was the famous daredevil Evel Knievel. We would get together on a Saturday afternoon and watch Evel Knievel jump his motorcycle on Wide World of Sports. The funny thing is, we were always hoping Evel would crash. We didn't want him to get killed but watching him crash was always fun! After watching an Evel Knievel jump on TV we would rush outside and get on the Big Wheel and pretend to crash just like the famous daredevil.

Chris actually lived in two different houses on Riverview Dr. In the summer of 1973, his parents rented a house at one end of the street and then in early 1976 they bought a house towards the other end of Riverview and moved into that house. Chris's dad was always friendly to me. He was an athletic man that enjoyed playing adult league softball and basketball. His dad had an office job in Shepherdsville. Occasionally, Chris and I would go to work with his dad and while his dad was working, we would walk around in Shepherdsville buying comic books or maybe some candy. Chris's mom was a very gentle, soft spoken lady who enjoyed playing tennis. I remember years later when Chris broke his neck in a freak diving accident how much she said she appreciated me coming to see him. She was a very sweet lady.

Once, Chris, Greg and I all camped out in the back of Greg's dad's van. We ran an extension cord out to the van so we could watch the show "Friday's" on TV. Years later the show would become a cult classic. Before the night started, Chris snuck into his parent's liquor cabinet and took a bottle of liquor. After we watched the show, we started drinking it, but we wanted more. So, Greg and I talked Chris into going back to his house and sneaking out another bottle. Obviously, this was a bad idea but, optimistic Greg reassured Chris that everything would workout. So, the three of us walked over to Chris's house. Greg and I waited outside on the carport while Chris snuck into the house to get us one more bottle of the old redeye. From outside, Greg and I could see Chris creeping slowly through the kitchen. We watched as he knelt down in front of the liquor cabinet and opened it, but suddenly unbeknownst to Chris, Greg and I could see the silhouette of Chris's mom standing at the doorway of the kitchen. There was no way for us to let Chris know it! All at once we heard, "Christopher Logan, just what are you doing?!!!!" She began yelling at him using a tone of voice I had never heard her use before. It was horrible, less then 20 feet from where we stood, Chris was being read the Riot Act by his mom. So, we did what all boys do under those circumstances, WE RAN AWAY! Heck, there was no reason for all of us to get in trouble, right?

As Oliver Hardy would say to Stan Laurel, "Well, here's another fine mess you've gotten us into!" The truth be told, I got Chris into far more messes then he got me into. He and I have now been friends for nearly 50 years. In a lot of ways, he hasn't changed much. Chris and I meet for lunch a few times a year. Each time we get together I am reminded of what great childhood friends I had. Chris Logan is most definitely one of them.

It's All Elementary

It was 1969, Joe Namath's New York Jets would pull off a huge upset to win the Super Bowl. Richard Nixon was the President of the United States. On July 20th of that year one of man's crowning achievements occurs when American astronaut Neil Armstrong became the first human to set foot on the Moon. A three-day rock concert known as the Woodstock Music Festival attracts more than 350,000 "hippies" to Yasgur's farm in New York. The Who, Janis Joplin, Joe Cocker, Crosby, Stills, Nash & Young and The Jimi Hendrix Experience were just some of the artists that performed. Surprisingly, the show would live up to its billing of "Three Days of Peace and Music." Then, later that fall I would enter the first grade at Roby Elementary School in Shepherdsville Kentucky.

If you went to elementary school in the early 1970's, then it's likely you would remember the following things. Fat pencils from first grade, chalkboard and erasers, the entire alphabet hanging on the wall above every chalkboard. Hand crank pencil sharpeners, Highlights and Dynamite magazines, lunch money, metal lunch boxes with thermoses. Textbooks and an American flag in every single classroom. Many things come to mind when I think of elementary school. One of my memories involved a ritual that took place in the classroom every morning. The teacher would ask the whole class to stand and face the American flag. Then, we would hold our right hand over our hearts and say, "I pledge allegiance to the Flag of the United States of America, and to the Republic for which it stands, one Nation under God, indivisible, with liberty and justice for all." That wasn't a bad way to start the day.

Yes, these are my earliest memories of going to school. It all started at Roby Elementary School in Shepherdsville Ky. In 1969 when I started first grade Mr. Masden was the principal of the school. He held that job until he retired in 1975. In 1976, Mr. Murphy would become the next principal. This can't be stated enough, when I was a boy, I hated school. It was just never easy for me. I could never identify with other friends of mine that enjoyed school. Of course, those kids were smart and made good grades. It always seemed as though school came easy to some kids. I struggled with it from the beginning all the way until the very end. When I was little, I would catch the bus at the end of the street. A bunch of us kids from the neighborhood would catch the bus there every morning. But, on the first day of school when I was in the first grade, my mom took me to school. My teacher was Mrs. Myers. I remember after I got to the classroom, they pinned a card on my shirt that had my teachers name and my bus number on it. They did that to every kid in the classroom. I'm sure that was done so they could keep track of all the little tikes running around. I was very nervous. I remember feeling somewhat lost without my brother Jerry there with me. Up to that point, Jerry was my closest companion and all at once I was put in a class with all these other kids and Jerry wasn't there for me to lean on. I was small for my age and as a child I was also very, very shy. Plus, because of having cerebral palsy I got picked on. In a short time, it would become apparent that I also had a learning disability that made it more difficult for me to learn at the same pace as my classmates. So, for me school just felt like a constant struggle. Up to that point my mom didn't work outside the home. After all of us kids were finally in school, she began to volunteer at school to help the slower kids with their class work. After she did this for a couple of years, they hired her as Volunteer Coordinator. Her job was to organize and coordinate all the parent and student volunteers. Occasionally, if I got sick, I would go to Mom's office and she would take me home. On occasion, I would pretend to be sick so I could stay home. Then I'd watch The Brady Bunch, The Mike Douglas Show and a few game shows. I learned not to fake it very often though because in our house there was a rule that if you were too sick to go to school then you were too sick to go outside and play. I usually didn't want to miss out on going out to play.

Even though I hated school, in the third grade I had perfect attendance. At the end of that year, my teacher (Mrs. Kite) gave me a card with a silver dollar in it to congratulate me. To this day, I still have that card and the silver dollar. It was to be the only year I ever had perfect attendance. I liked Mrs. Kite and she was also one of Mom's good friends.

Few things stand out more in one's memory then lunchtime at school. Most of the time, I took my lunch. Mom got me a lunchbox that was red, white and blue and shaped like a mailbox. It had "US Mail" painted on the side of it. She would make my lunch each day and I always looked forward to it. With baited enthusiasm, I would sit down at the lunchroom table and unlatch my mailbox lunchbox. As I opened it, the warm smell of what was inside would instantly warm my soul. I would find a peanut butter and jelly sandwich carefully wrapped ever so neatly with wax paper. A small bag of Cheetos, a banana and a couple of delicious HoHo's for dessert. All of this put together with nothing more than Mom's love. To a 4th grader, that was better than a steak dinner!

In the 4th grade I had Mr. Silverman. He was one of my favorite teachers. He was very patient with me. He also had a cage with a couple of gerbils in it in his classroom. For a little boy like me, I thought that was cool. The part about school that I hated the most were oral book reports or anytime they called on me to read out loud to the whole class. Because of my poor reading skills and my shyness, I would nearly make myself sick anytime I was made to read to the class. I don't miss that part of school at all.

Occasionally, my dad would take a day off work for one thing or another. Whenever he was home in the morning, he would take great joy in waking Jerry and I up for school. Dad would come busting into our bedroom singing something like, "It's time to get up, it's time to get up, it's time to get up in the morning!" Jerry and I would be sound asleep and in no mood for a song and dance routine from someone that could neither sing nor dance. Dad sure enjoyed teasing us in that way though.

For the 6th grade I had Mrs. Stonehurst. She was very patient with me and she clearly loved children. She seemed to pay close attention to me. My best friends during that time were Dan Taylor and Archie O'Malley.

Dan knew how to play the guitar and I thought that was very cool. In the 6th grade he could play "Smoke on The Water" by Deep Purple. Years later, he became a very good banjo player and had his own bluegrass band. My other best friend was Archie O'Malley and he lived down the street from me. Archie was just crazy about Godzilla, Elvis, Bruce Lee and the Civil War. He was interesting to say the least.

My last year of elementary school was the bicentennial year of 1976. It was a central event in the memory of the American Revolution. The Bicentennial culminated on Sunday, July 4, 1976, with the 200th anniversary of the adoption of the Declaration of Independence. Back in 1976, the Bicentennial was a huge event and led to many celebrations for the entire year. There were Bicentennial parades, firework shows and revolutionary war reenactments and other celebrations all throughout the country. For me, I was just a kid who was trying to survive my 7th grade year and my last year of elementary school. My 7th grade teacher was Mr. Pendergast. My best friend in class that year was Chet Steelman. Chet had been in special ed classes because he was a little slow and had recently been put into regular classes. While in the seventh grade Chet was about 15 years old. That meant he was considerably bigger than all the other boys in class. At the time, there were 2 boys in particular that would bully me every chance they got. Their names were Doug Porter and Tommy Mullins. After I befriended Chet, if they picked on me then Chet would literally beat the crap out of both of them. I was the smallest kid in class and Chet was by far the biggest. He always protected me. Chet was a great guy. During recess, we would sit outside on the school yard while facing the interstate and Chet would say, "One day I'm gonna be driving a big truck like that down the road." Being that those were the days of CB radios and songs about truckers, it was easy for boys to dream about driving big trucks. Chet was a genuinely good guy and a wonderful friend. Many, many years later I would learn that Chet was indeed driving one of those gigantic trucks at a rock quarry for a living.

After seven long years, I had finally reached the end of elementary school. The next year I would begin a whole new journey at a new school.

That school would be bigger and more intimidating then Roby Elementary. I was moving on to Shepherdsville Junior High. It would provide more challenges and new friends. But first, there were the dog days of summer to enjoy. Doing important things like building a clubhouse in Baker's backyard with a group of friends. Setting off fireworks. Playing pickup basketball on Shannon Weaver's driveway or riding on the back of his XR 75 dirt bike while he raced through the field behind our neighborhood. Other activities included having water balloon fights, playing manhunt, riding my bike until dark and noticing dirty magazines for the first time. There was also camping out and getting into mischief.

Being that I detested school so much, I always looked forward to summertime because if it were summer then I was out of school. About midway through the summer break each year, Dad would start the long countdown to the first day of school. It would go something like this After
a long summer day of running around on our bikes, we would ride back to my house. As my friends and I would ride up the driveway, my dad and Mr. Phelps would be seated on the front porch. My dad would take great pleasure in shouting, "Hey boys, 28 days until school starts!" All of my friends would answer with a loud grown and say something like, "Oh Mr. Huckaby, we don't want to hear that." My dad and Mr. Phelps would then bust into laughter. The next day, he would surprise us again with the same statement all over again, only this time he would remove a day from the day before "Hey boys, 27 days until school starts!"

Soon, my summer days would run out and it would be time for school to start all over again. Back then, little did I know just how fleeting those days would be. In just 7 short years I was finished with elementary school. In the fall, I would be moving on to junior high school. I would continue to struggle but I would learn to never give up.

Square Dancing! (Can it get any Worse?)

If you were a little boy growing up in the 1970's, then you were convinced that all girls had cooties which meant that you would never want to be around them. Unless of course, you thought one of them was cute! Talk about confusing times. With that in mind, during my 5th grade school year something horrible happened. Every kid in the 5th grade, boys & girls alike, was taken to the school cafeteria. Then it was announced that we were all going to be forced to square dance with each other. SQUARE DANCE?! Yes, SQUARE DANCE! All anyone could think was YUCK! To start off this awful event, we were told to line up so we could be matched up with our dance partner. That's right, you would begin with this very awkward and uncomfortable nightmare of having your dance partner picked for you. To make matters even worse, the person that organized and headed up this whole escapade just so happened to be a very mean teacher. Her name was Mrs. Weidermeyer. She had a head full of silver hair and it was always up in a bun. She was an old school, corporal punishment type of teacher. Mrs. Weidermeyer actually wore a police whistle around her neck at school every day. The woman would blow it at ear splitting decibels just to get the full attention of her classroom. She would also grab the big, wooden door of her classroom and slam it loud and hard to strike the fear of God into her students. She was known to exhibit a few strict disciplinary tactics on her students as well. If you were caught talking during her class, she just might get your attention by reaching out and yanking your ear or she would even pinch you. Believe it or not, Mrs. Weidermeyer was the person my elementary school put in charge of square dancing. Sometimes, if there were an odd number of boys then some poor 5th grade boy would have to dance with Mrs. Weidermeyer. When you're a little boy, nothing, and I mean nothing could be worse than square dancing, unless you were also unlucky enough to be forced to square dance with one of the meanest teachers in the whole school. Heck, even dancing with a 5th grade girl that you feared might be covered with cooties would be a better option then dancing with Warden Weidermeyer.

More than 20 years later, I began going to Clermont Baptist Church and I noticed Mrs. Weidermeyer was the organist. After going there for a while, I realized that Mrs Weidermeyer had softened a little in her old age. An older gentleman at church suffered from crippling arthritis in his hands. One Sunday morning Mrs. Weidermeyer was going into church. As she rushed past the old gentlemen, she stopped to shake his hand. The man cringed in pain, then turned toward another member and said, "My goodness, that woman has a grip like a prizefighter!" It just goes to prove that if someone was as hard as Mrs. Weidermeyer was then they might not even know that their crushing the hand of an arthritis sufferer. He should just be glad he never had to square dance with her!

Ghosts and Goblins in the 1970's

This is a nostalgic look back at the Halloween from yesteryear. When I was a kid, Halloween was a big deal. During the 70's Halloween was at the height of its popularity. Just ask anyone that grew up back then and they will tell you how much more exciting it was then compared to now. I think Halloween was the only holiday that was entirely made just for kids. Watching "It's the Great Pumpkin, Charlie Brown", "Frankenstein", or "The Ghost and Mr. Chicken" starring Don Knotts would surely put any kid in the mood for ghosts and goblins. Halloween was about homemade costumes, plastic fangs and vampire blood. It was about silly ghosts, spooky witches and black cats. It was about jack o lanterns, cheap plastic masks and plenty of candy. Halloween was also all about going trick or treating. Trick or treating was important stuff to a kid back then. I look back fondly on my Halloween memories as a young kid growing up in 1970s suburban America. Once, I remember getting dressed up like a vampire and going trick or treating with my brother Jerry and a few other neighborhood kids. In those days, the parents stayed home to give out candy and you got with a few friends and ran the neighborhood knocking on doors. Filling our pillowcase's with candy, I remember how excited we were and how far we'd roam. The streets were crawling with kids just like us and laughter was heard everywhere. Unlike today, back then every porch in the neighborhood proudly displayed their own hand carved jack o lantern. One house might have a black light replacing their porch light. That was always cool! By 10pm on Halloween night, my friends and I would often find ourselves what seemed like a mile or two away from our own homes. By nights end, we would take our pillowcase's full of candy back home and sift through it to check out just how rich our candy fortune was. It was all there, everything from Pixie sticks, Kit Kat bars, Bubble Gum, Bottle Caps, 3 Musketeers, M&M's, Reese Cups, Payday's, Mr. Goodbar's, Sweet Tarts, Milky Ways, Crunch Bars and my favorite candy bar of all, Snickers. Not all the candy was the good stuff though. You would also end up with that hard crap called "candy corn". I think candy corn was nothing more than shards of plastic that had been spray painted orange and yellow. They had an overly sweet deodorant-flavored taste. Try eating a small candle or some earwax and you've had candy corn. Then there were also those awful orange circus peanuts. The oversized peanut shaped candy felt more like you were eating foam rubber then candy. Those things were in a nasty class all their own.

When I reached the point that I was too old to trick or treat, Halloween became all about getting into mischief. In 1973 a movie came out titled "Walking Tall". The film was based on the life of Tennessee Sheriff Buford Pusser. While carrying a big stick Sheriff Pusser almost single-handily cleaned up his small town of crime and corruption. As kids, we thought the stick wielding sheriff was cool. Back then, there was an old graveyard several yards behind my house. We found a big stick back there and we whittled all the bark off of it, so it looked like Sheriff Buford Pusser's stick from the movie. Since we thought it was no longer cool to trick or treat, we decided to go out late on Halloween night and smash pumpkin's and jack o lanterns with our newly carved stick. Yes, this is the kind of mischief that 13-year-old boys get into whenever they think they are too old to trick or treat. It's like a midlife crisis for kids only it's a mid-kid-crisis. You're too old to trick or treat but your too young to drive. So, you lash out with totally ridiculous and mischievous behavior. I think it's also looked at as, becoming a mindless teenager, but boy it was fun.

As a teenager, I would sometimes be the one left to give out candy. Once, I handed out candy with a few friends. We never liked the trick or treaters that were driven around by their parents. Most of them were driven in from Louisville. So, we decided to give out candy to the walking trick or treaters but the ones that were being driven from door to door, they were given a handful of gravel. Obviously, it just goes to show that it's never a good idea to leave the important job of handing out candy to teenage boys, especially if you want it done right.

The old, overgrown graveyard behind my house was more than a hundred years old. It was the Simmons family cemetery. It seemed more like an overgrown forest with a few graves sprinkled around. One of the deceased was that of Jamie Simmons who's grave had a rod iron fence around it. As kids, we would frequently play in the old graveyard. We would play manhunt or sometimes just go there to hangout. A couple of times, we went there and sat in a circle around the old Simmons grave to have a seance. After lighting a candle, I would be a little creeped out before we even got started. As we sat there in total silence, the first snap of a twig or gust of the wind and we would all jump up screaming and run out of there. You just knew if you were unlucky enough to fall down, none of your friends would stop to help you. They would have just left you there to be eaten by the old Simmons ghost. So much for being friends until the end!

By our teenage years we decided to make our own haunted house in one of my friend's basement. His name was Mike White. We spent a few days decorating the basement up with a cardboard coffin and other ghoulish things to make it nice and spooky. On Halloween night, we dressed up in scary makeup, then we escorted some willing trick or treaters down in the basement. At just the right time, one of us would jump out of that coffin and scare the pee out of them. Yes, these were the glory days of Halloween. It's easy to be nostalgic about Halloween from the 1970's. The smart phone kids and the Facebook kids of this generation will never know how much fun Halloween once was. Back then kids used their imagination to create more fun for themselves. During the golden age of Halloween, it was a wonderful time to be a kid.

Summer Means Fun

When I was 10, I met a boy named Archie O'Malley. He lived in a house at the end of Riverview Drive. Archie and I were the same age and over time we became best friends. When I first met Archie, he was crazy about Godzilla and other old monster movies. At the time, he had a Godzilla model and a few other vintage Hasbro monster models. Keeping with the Asian theme, Archie was really into Bruce Lee and Ultraman as well. He also had a collection of silent super 8 movies. Most of them were Japanese monster movies. Those old 200 ft. movies were 10 minutes long and he would watch them on a hand crank movie editor. It had about a 3" screen. I didn't mind that small screen because I was just blown away that he had something that he could watch those movies on anytime he wanted right in his own bedroom. You must keep in mind that this was years before VCR's or Blue-ray players. Back then, the only way to watch a movie in your home was to wait until it came on television. So, to me, the fact that he could watch those little movies anytime he wanted was just the coolest thing. I had never seen anything like it before and I wanted one. Eventually over time, I had my own collection of super 8 movies only mine were of The Marx Brothers, Abbott & Costello, Frankenstein and Dracula. The first super 8 movie my mom ever got me was Star Wars. She got it in the PX at Fort Knox. I also had a collection of little hand painted civil war soldiers that my mom got me for Christmas and Archie had some too. He and I would get together and play with them. A few years later, I ended up trading Archie for all of his super 8 movies and for his civil war soldiers. I still have them.

Archie and I got along well together. A few of us guys built a clubhouse in the corner of Archie's back yard. We worked on it after we got home from school. Archie's dad would come home from work while we were building it. He would always walk back there and say, "This place looks like a damn Mongolian shit house!!!" How a man raised in rural Kentucky ever came up with a phrase like that is a mystery to me. To say that his dad was a character would be an understatement. His dad liked to play the fiddle. He was actually pretty good at it but when you're a kid, you're not impressed by hearing a middle-aged man play bluegrass on a fiddle. Archie's mom's name was Margaret. She was an attractive middle-aged lady with a bad temper. Occasionally, she would unleash that temper on Archie. Margaret could be rather colorful as well. In the mid 1970's Margaret really got into disco music. Back then, I hated disco, but nowadays when I compare it to rap music, I think disco music wasn't that bad. Archie's mom & dad would do fun things with us. I remember they took us the see "Smokey and the Bandit" at the drive-in. That was fun.

Sometimes Archie and I would stay all night with each other. In the 1970's, there was a huge CB radio craze and Archie's mom listened to a CB radio or a scanner a lot. Occasionally, when I would stay all night with Archie, the scanner/CB radio would play throughout the house all night long. It was very annoying, and it would be hard for me to sleep. Obviously, they were used to it and they never seemed bothered by it. Sometimes, Archie would stay all night at my house. Once after Elvis died, Archie stayed all night at my house, and we did something odd in honor of Elvis. Archie and and I took an old Johnny West action figure and painted big sideburns on it to make it resemble Elvis. Then we fixed a metal box up to look like a coffin and we put our hand painted Elvis in it. Then we buried him in Archie's yard. Without question, that was a very odd thing to do.

Archie and I both had some electric trains. On cold winter days, he would bring his over and we would set them all up and play with them together. When we were in junior high school Archie loved professional wrestling. I enjoyed watching it some too, but Archie was just crazy about it. Tojo Yamamoto, Jimmy Hart, Billy Dundee, Jimmy Valiant and of course, Jerry "The King" Lawler were all wrestlers that we watched back then. After watching it, Archie would get all excited and wrestle his little brother all over the living room floor. He was known to get carried away while wrestling and get a little too rough and cause real pain. Once he threw his little brother against the wall knocking a big hole in the wall. He liked to find an unsuspecting, naive guy and do the figure four leg lock on them.

He was just a little too into that stuff. Archie continued to really enjoy watching wrestling well into his late teens to early 20's but, I had long outgrown it by then. You could say that Archie didn't have an interest in things, Archie was obsessed with things. He would go from one obsession to another. One of his obsessions was civil war reenactments. I think this one started earlier in his childhood. My first memory of Archie was of us pretending we were in the civil war and we were confederate soldiers. He always wanted us to be confederate soldiers and I just went along with it. I'm not sure why because I'm not a racist and I always thought slavery was wrong. Maybe I was a closet union soldier. Ha! Archie didn't appear to be a racist either. Maybe he just liked the gray confederate uniforms better then the Yankee blue uniforms. Archie would later really get into participating in civil war reenactments. Playing army with a bunch of grown men seemed very strange to me. I once participated in a civil war reenactment with him, but it just wasn't my kind of thing. Plus, buying the stuff could be rather expensive.

Archie and I both enjoyed collecting things together. We would go to the flea markets and record conventions and he would look for Jan & Dean records and I would look for records by The Who. That was always lots of fun. Archie also learned how to play the bass guitar. He could play "I Got You" by the Split Enz, "Burnin' For You" by Blue Oyster Cult and "Time Won't Let Me" by The Outsiders. Archie was shy and he lacked confidence in his playing, so he never wanted to play it anywhere except his own bedroom. He did seem to enjoy playing his bass though.

Over time, I got close to Archie's Grandmother and his Great Grandmother. His Grandmother would make Archie a german chocolate cake from scratch for his birthday and it was delicious. She was a great cook and a truly wonderful lady. Years later, his Great Grandmother would become a huge influence on me after I became a Christian.

When Archie and I started high school, we walked to school together everyday. When I would get to his house every morning, his mom would be fixing him and his brother a full breakfast complete with eggs, bacon, hash browns and toast. All I got for breakfast before school was a bowl of Cheerios. Ha! Sometimes, Archie and his brother would nearly come to blows over who got the last piece of toast or bacon.

Not only did Archie and I walk to school together, we walked and rode our bikes on the streets of our neighborhood hundreds of times over the years. We would walk to football games in the fall and basketball games in the winter. As fate would have it, Archie and I would even end up walking the line side by side on graduation day to get our diploma's together. I thought that was really neat. I would also go on to be a groomsman in his wedding.

Archie was a great guy to grow up with. He was naive and gullible to a fault, but he was also very dedicated to his friends. He added a great deal of fun and laughter to my childhood. My memories of Archie always make me smile. After growing up, Jack married his teenage sweetheart. They would go on to have 2 kids. It was a blast having Archie as a friend while growing up on Riverview Drive.

The House is Rockin'

When I was about 13, I met a guy named Randy Miller. Randy's mom was from the Philippines and his dad was from the United States. His dad had been killed in Vietnam. Randy and I became best friends. My earliest memories of Randy are of how artistic he was. Randy could make anything out of cardboard. He once made a miniature Skylab and space shuttle both out of cardboard and wire. They were about 6" long. They looked as good as a plastic model. That was just the beginning of what he would go on to make.

Randy was the first friend I ever had that was as crazy about music as I was. We would go to concerts together. The first concert I ever went to was to see Triumph. We would go on to see The Who, REO Speedwagon, UFO, Ozzy Osbourne, 38 Special and more. We really enjoyed seeing a live show. Randy and I both loved the band Cheap Trick. Back when we were making our super 8 movies, he and I got this great idea of filming a short live performance of ourselves dressed up like the members of Cheap Trick. I would help him make all the instruments, including the whole drum set out of cardboard. Rodney set out to make a full-size red explorer guitar that was identical to the one Rick Nielsen played. I would get to play Rick in our film. He then made a wood grain telecaster guitar identical to the one Robin Zander played and a 12-string bass just like the one Tom Petersson played. Then he set out to make a full-size Bun E. Carlos drum set. Randy lived two streets over from me. We would carry that red explorer guitar back and forth from my house to Randy's house. People would stop and say, "I didn't know you played the guitar!" I would say, "I don't play guitar, this one is made out of cardboard." It was neat to me that people started thinking I could play guitar. Randy was just so artistic that he could make a guitar out of cardboard that looked that realistic. We would work on making the instruments during the day and at night we would go into Randy's garage and jam with them. We would turn up the stereo, put on some live Cheap Trick and pretend we were the members of the band. I know it seems corny but, as kids we would just have a blast pretending to play those cardboard instruments with ear busting music playing! As it turned out, we got tired of all the detail work of making all the instruments and we couldn't find anyone to play the other 2 members of the band. So, we asked my friend Archie to come over and film us playing the song "Surrender" as we just destroyed all of the instruments in a fit of teenage fury.

Erin Gray was an actress that starred in Buck Rogers in the 25th Century. Randy and I watched that show just to see Erin walking around in that tight jumpsuit. Obviously at that time, Randy and I were a couple of typical teenage boys just going through puberty, so we had the hots for actress Erin Gray. Well, in the early 80's Erin Gray was at the Carl Casper Car Show. So, we went to the show. We had to go and get her autograph. Randy and I got in that long line to get Erin's autograph. It was hot and there were a lot of people smoking. As I stood there in line, the heat and the smoke began to make me nauseous. I said, "Randy, I don't feel very well. I think I'm gonna be sick." Randy said, "What? You're getting ready to meet Erin Gray! You can't get sick!" I said, "Let me go up first so I can get it over with." Randy let me go first so I rushed up on the stage to where she was seated behind a small table. I handed her the picture I had for her to sign and I asked her to sign it. She said, "How would you like for me to sign it?" From how my stomach was churning, I knew I didn't have long so I said, "Oh, I don't care, just sign it" Then she said, "What is your name?" I knew I would blow at any second, so I said, "JUST SIGN IT!!!!" She signed her name to it, and I grabbed it and rushed off of the stage. Then, with a loud groan and a big splash, I threw up all over the floor! It was nasty and loud. I have no doubt she heard me. Randy came off the stage just behind me and said, "GROSS! Let's get out of here!" After that, I never attempted to meet anymore Hollywood actresses. I figured; God only knows what else could happen.

Back then, my mom and dad would go to the Commissary at Fort Knox to get groceries. My mom would get these little brown frozen donuts that you warm in the toaster oven. Randy would stay the night and I would warm up those donuts. We loved them. They were delicious! We would stay up late, and I would warm up those donuts and we'd watch Midnight Special and Don Kirshner's Rock Concert. We would have a great time! At other times we'd stay up and record The King Biscuit Flower Hour on WLRS late night radio. It came on at midnight every Saturday night. That show would showcase a different live performance every week. From Cheap Trick, Pat Benatar, Meat Loaf, Loverboy to Queen and everything in between. It was fun stuff to listen to. We would stay up nearly all-night drawing posters to hang on the walls in my bedroom. One of them was of The Who playing live. The members were drawn as cartoon characters. Another one we drew was of Pink Floyd, "The Wall" and also one of Rainbow live on stage. These took a lot of late nights and they were a lot of fun. I still have them displayed on the wall in the basement.

As we got older, Randy would buy a real drum set and I would buy a Sunn PA system and we tried to put our own band together. The band was called Rapid Fire. But, in a short time it became obvious that I couldn't sing, so I gave up and sold the PA to Randy. To me, the cardboard guitars were far more fun to play anyway. Ha!

Randy came along during a time in my childhood when I needed someone like him. We both had the same kind of adolescent problems. Neither one of us was popular at school. Neither one of us could get any attention from girls and we both liked hard rock music. We leaned on each other during some tough times. We both felt like outcasts, but we had each other. We became best friends. Randy was a leg man and I was a butt man. We would see a pretty lady in a dress, and he would say, 'Wow, look at her legs!" And I would say, "Yeah, but look at her butt!" Ha! Later, on our lives would go in different directions and he joined the Marines. I was happy for him. I wish him nothing but the very best. His friendship will always be special to me. It's funny how when you're a kid you think you will always be friends with your best friends then you get older and you drift so far apart. It's as if you were never friends with that person at all. Randy sure left me with some awesome memories and for that I'm truly grateful. After all, isn't that what having a friend is all about?

You're in the Army now!

This is one of those stories that you hear about that sounds fictional, but it really happened. It's about my friend Archie. To say that Archie was naive and gullible would be a huge understatement. That meant he was a prime candidate for a practical joke. Well, this is a crazy story about a practical joke that got blown way out of proportion. It started from nothing more than just playing on my friend Jack's fears of the draft. Archie and I were the same age and during our early childhood, the United States still drafted young men into the military. Archie and I were both just 10 years old in 1973 when the draft ended. After that, young people joined the selective service on their own and they were not forced to do so. Five or six years later Archie would still worry that they would reinstate the draft again and he would be called to go and serve his country. Back when there was a draft, a young man had to be 18 years old to be drafted. Even though Archie was only 16 at the time, my friend Randy and I came up with the silly idea of sending Archie a fake draft noticed. We batted this crazy idea around wondering if he would fall for it. We decided to try out our prank to see if it would work on our insanely gullible friend. It took a little work to pull off our practical joke. Since neither I nor Randy could type very well, we enlisted the help of Randy's older sister to type the fictitious draft notice for us. In so many words, it said that Archie was being drafted and that he was to report for duty on such and such date to Fort Knox Ky. To make it look official we needed the American seal stamped on it but, we didn't have one. In the end, Randy drew the American seal on the draft notice by hand. We then put Archie's name and address on it and put it in the mail.

The next morning, I went to see Randy and we walked over to Archie's house to see if he had received the notice. Well, we were blown away by what happened next. We knocked on the door and suddenly Archie's dad hurriedly rushed out the door holding his sons draft notice in his fisted hand. He was furious and cussing up a storm. He said, "My boy's been drafted and I ain't gonna stand for this S#@t! He told us that Archie wasn't home. He then said, "Archie is about to go ape S#@T! I'm taking this here draft notice down to the damn post office and I'm gonna get to the bottom of this S#@T!" He was very animated, pacing back and forth. He shook his fist and yelled "I'm gonna sue the F@#%*n' government, that's what I'm gonna do! Those assholes are not drafting my boy!" Randy and I were speechless. We knew if Archie's dad took that fake draft notice to the post office that we could be in big trouble. So, we needed to find Archie and fast.

I would later find out that as soon as Archie found out he was being drafted, he rushed to his friend Kurt McCray's house to tell him. Kurt would later tell me that Jack showed up first thing that morning beating on his door and panicked out of his mind saying, "Kurt, I've been drafted!" Obviously, Kurt smelled a rat right away and he tried to tell Archie that something had to be up since there was no longer a draft in our country, but Archie would have none of it. As crazy as it sounds, Archie was thoroughly convinced that he was being drafted.

Randy and I walked over to one of Archie's other friends house, his name was Chester Rutherford. From a distance, we could see Archie was on Chester's porch with Kurt and Chester. We could see from several yards away that Archie was upset. He was pacing back and forth flailing his arms in the air saying, "I've been drafted! What am I gonna do?!" As we were walking up, I said, "Archie, we've got something to tell you   "
With that Kurt said, "IT WAS YOU GUYS!" and then he busted into boisterous laughter. We confessed and came clean for the nasty practical joke we had played on him. Archie was furious and saw nothing funny about it. At the same time, Kurt was literally laying on the porch laughing uncontrollably. Chester began taking up for Archie while telling Randy and I what a terrible thing we had done. Archie yelled at us while Kurt just continued to laugh himself silly. All in all, it was an unforgettable afternoon.

In the end, Randy and I were forbidden to go over to Archie's house for several months by his parents. The story of that practical joke became legendary. I think what made it the stuff of legend was that Archie's whole family believed it. They are good people. They were just incredibly naive and gullible. After everything was said and done, we all remained friends. It was just a silly practical joke that became neighborhood folklore. At the very beginning, Randy and I questioned whether-or-not Archie would even fall for our little prank. What were we thinking?

Greg Time

Greg was always optimistic. Greg was very driven. Greg had an outrageous, silly sense of humor. Greg was a very loyal friend. These are all true statements about my childhood friend, Greg Collins. We met when I was about 13. I was two years older than him. My earliest memory of Greg is of playing basketball with him and Shannon Weaver on Shannon's driveway. I was terrible at basketball, but I still played with them. Greg and I were both big Minnesota Vikings football fans. This was during the 1970's when the Vikings had Fran Tarkenton, Chuck Foreman, Ahmad Rashād and the purple people eaters defense. The Vikings had lost 4 Super Bowls during that time. It was tough being a fan because they could never win the big one. Greg and I were also big Louisville Cardinal fans as well. His dad was a Kentucky Wildcat fan. Greg and I would get together with his dad and watch the Kentucky vs. Louisville game. We would tease his dad incessantly over every loss Kentucky would have against any opponent. Greg's dad would do the same thing to us anytime Louisville lost a game. Greg and I even had 2 Indiana hats that we would wear on the day of the Kentucky vs. Indiana game just to irritate his dad. All in good fun, of course.

Greg's dad and my dad became friends as well. My dad was very strict and very blunt. I think most of my friends in the neighborhood were intimidated, if not just downright afraid of my dad. Most of them except Greg. No matter what my dad did or said, Greg just thought my dad was hilarious. At first, I didn't know what to make of Greg laughing at him, even if my dad were disciplining me. I think he just looked at my dad more like a character in a cartoon. Almost as if he were thinking to himself, "Is this man for real?" Which might explain why Greg and my friend Archie didn't get along very well. Greg would irritate Archie on purpose. That would make Archie angry. Archie too was like a cartoon character when he lost his temper. Archie would overreact and Greg thought it was funny, so he would continue to push his buttons. Greg would make him so mad that Archie would literally be chasing Greg all over the yard in anger. Greg would be laughing the whole time.

As teenagers, Greg and I had vastly different musical tastes. At the time I was into heavy metal music. He wasn't a fan of heavy metal. Greg enjoyed new wave music. I wasn't a fan of most new wave. I liked stuff like Ozzy Osbourne and AC/DC. Greg liked The Police, King Crimson and The Cars. The first time I ever heard Prince was in Greg's bedroom. I think Prince was his favorite.

We had vastly different tastes in art as well. I enjoyed drawing people from looking at photographs of them. The challenge was to make my drawing look as close to the picture as possible. To Greg, that wasn't art. Greg really enjoyed Impressionist art from artist like Claude Monet. Greg was very interested in art while he was in high school. He designed and painted a huge mural on the wall of the school cafeteria. It remained on the wall for several years. He worked on it all summer with Mr. Hefner, the art teacher. Mr. Hefner looked a lot like The Who guitarist Pete Townshend.

Greg was always willing to help. I was late learning how to ride a bike. I guess because I have cerebral palsy. My friends would always tote me on their bikes. My mom told me if I learned to ride a bike that she would buy me one for my birthday. When I told Greg what my mom said, he quickly took it as a challenge. He said, 'WOW! There is nothing to it! You can learn to ride on my old bike." Greg had an old stingray bike that he didn't ride anymore. By then he was riding a 10-speed bike. So, I went down to Greg's house and began practicing on his old bike. I would get on it and ride a short distance then fall over. I would try it again. Over and over and over and over again I would crash. He kept telling me I could do it. I just kept trying to ride again and again until something clicked, and I got it. I could FINALLY ride a bike. I got on that bike and rode it down the street to my house to show Mom I had learned to ride. My parents were sitting out on the porch. When I came riding up, the expression on my mom's face was priceless. True to her word, Mom got me a bike for my birthday. That wouldn't have happened without Greg's constant encouragement. Greg never doubted for a second that I would learn how to ride a bike.

A few years later while in college, Greg would write a paper on me and my learning disability. For years I had been so ashamed of my poor reading and spelling skills that I had hidden it. When I finally opened to Greg, he encouraged me to do something about it. He got me an electronic spell checker. I carried that thing everywhere and used it so much that I wore it out. With a lot of encouragement from Greg, I enrolled in a remedial reading program at the public library. In a few weeks my reading greatly improved. I still had a lot of room for improvement but, it was a start. When I finished the program, I no longer felt dumb. Greg played a huge role in helping me to confront that problem head on and do something about it.

Greg was so full of optimism that he used to think he could get just about anything done in a short amount of time. Everything from mowing the yard, cutting a tree down and haul it away, changing the oil in his truck, go get a haircut, paint his bedroom and still have time to go for a run. In his mind, all of these things take about 30 minutes each. I would say, you can't get all that done in a day. He would say, "Yeah, I can." I would say, "That's Greg time". Of course, he would run out of time. Obviously, the scenario I used was a bit of an exaggeration. The point I was making is that he was a very positive guy who believed all things were possible. That is a great quality to have because he would always get a lot of things done.

Greg's dad was the Principal of North Bullitt High School. He was a good, hard working man. Just like his son, he loved a good practical joke. He enjoyed teasing me every chance he got. When he wasn't working, you would find him fishing, watching the Kentucky Wildcats, asleep on the couch or watching Andy Griffith. Even though I never went, his dad always encouraged me to go to college. Greg's parents were very supportive of him. I never felt that in my own home. Greg's mom was a religious lady.

Greg loved to scare his mom out of her wits on a regular basis. He might hide right before she would walk into a room and then jump out and scare the daylight's out of her. Once we walked in and found his mom sleeping in a chair right next to the vacuum cleaner. Greg turned to me and put his index finger in front of his mouth and said, "Shhhhh". Then he snuck over and proceeded to gently wrap the vacuum cleaner cord around his mom in the chair. When he was finished, he had literally tied his mom to the chair she was sleeping in with the vacuum cleaner cord. Then he quietly plugged the vacuum cleaner in. Then he pushed the 'on' button. The vacuum started with a loud roar and Mrs. Collins let out a deafening scream! She struggled to get out of the chair, but she couldn't. She yelled, "Gregory Thomas, let me up! This isn't funny!" Of course, at that point, Greg was just bent over laughing hysterically. That is just one of many practical jokes that Greg would play on his unsuspecting parents over the years.

Of course, things weren't always funny. As adults, Greg and I would both lose our dad's within months of each other. Both died from cancer. We leaned on each other all the way through it.

Greg always had a huge passion to help kids and to be around kids. I was afraid that he wouldn't find the right lady to have a family with. Like me, Greg didn't find his soulmate until he was in his 40's. She was young and beautiful, and she fulfilled his lifelong dream of having kids. It's no surprise that he is an outstanding father to his 3 children. His dad would be so proud to know that Greg would go on to become the woman's basketball coach at Western Kentucky University. WKU was his dad's and his alma mater.

Greg and I are still good friends. For more than 40 years, Greg has been there through the good times and the bad times. He has been there to help me through the death of both of my parents and he was there to experience the joy of watching me marry my long-awaited wife. A true friend can be hard to find. I have lived long enough to know that isn't something you take for granted. With all the twists and turns of life, to keep a friend of 40 plus years would have to be rare. Greg has been a constant source of friendship and support, but I also know to stay on my toes because with Greg around, I could be the butt of a practical joke at any time. That is not a bad price to pay to have a friend for a lifetime.

Camping in the Suburbs

When I was just a kid, I camped out with a few friends in the backyard for the first time. We just used an old army pup tent that had belonged to my brother Biff. All I knew was, it was fun, and I was hooked. After that I would continue to camp out somewhere in the neighborhood with an assortment of friends, for a few years to come. One of the fondest memories I have of camping was of a few of my friends lying in the tent and all of us singing "Country Roads" and "Poems, Prayers & Promises" acapella. And we sang "Rocky Top" acapella as well.

One reason we enjoyed camping out was it gave us more freedom to do stuff that we had no business doing. Stuff like walking the neighborhood at 2 or 3 in the morning. Stuff like throwing rocks at a teenage girl's window hoping to wake her up. Stuff like streaking. Streaking became a huge fad in the country during the summer of 1974. Yes, we would camp out and go streaking. Looking back, why a bunch of boys would think it would be fun to strip down and run around outside naked is beyond me. But, for whatever reason we thought it was fun at the time.

Camping was all about doing whatever you wanted. When you're 12, there is something dangerous, magical and intoxicating about walking through the empty streets with my friends in the middle of the night. One of my earliest memories camping out was with a few of my friends sneaking out after it got late and walking a few streets over to old man Wedemeyer's house. Old man Wedemeyer had a garden that was across from Bullitt Central High School. Well, one night we stole a huge watermelon from his garden. It was way too big to carry so we rolled it most of the way home. Which so happened to be about three streets from where we were camping, and it was a long way to be rolling a watermelon.

Whenever we finally got it home, we busted it open and ate it. There was another neighbor down the street that raised a few strawberries and we would sneak down there and eat them right off the vine. I guess it was the thrill of getting caught. Once, Randy and I tied a bunch of cans on the back of Mr. Mitchell's truck and when he left for work about 5:00 a.m. he went driving off down the road making a ton of noise dragging those cans behind him. Another time Randy and I filled the Mitchell's birdbath with Cheerios and then put a spoon in it. Once, we even tied fishing line to a neighbor's front bumper and tied the other end to their porch chairs. Obviously, the neighbors weren't happy with us. We were just high- spirited boys having innocent fun. We would mostly do mischievous things like that, but we weren't all about mischief though. We did fun innocent things a lot of the time too. We enjoyed old black & white movies. One time we ran an extension cord out to the tent so we could watch an old
W.C. Fields movie that came on late. We would also take a projector out there and watch our super 8 movies. Occasionally, we would light the grill and roast hotdogs and marshmallows.

Whenever we got a little older, we would camp out and walk to the Convenient store and I would watch Greg and Randy play video games like Defender or Pac Man. Then we would either pick out some tasty frozen pizza to put into the store microwave or get some junk food. Sometimes I would buy a rock and roll magazine there as well.

My camping out stories of silliness and mischief are endless, these are just a few. It was a wonderful way for a boy to spend his summer nights, hanging out with my friends and making memories. The events of childhood are never completely clear. Years later, my camping stories seemed more like epic adventures then just stories. Growing up can be very hard at times. It can be kind of like a series of battles. Everything from blackheads and puberty to peer pressure and bullying. It's a minefield of hard knocks. Well, if growing up is a battle then those friends who grew up with you deserve respect because they were down in the trenches of childhood with you. Those true friends stood by you during a time when you had no idea what tomorrow would bring and your whole life lay before you. They were not just part of the silly mischief of your childhood, they played an important role that would help mold you into the adult you would later become. Those friends would also leave you with special memories that you would continue to carry with you for the rest of your life.

The Great Pumpkin Caper

During the fall of 1979 my friend Greg and I decided to play an elaborate Halloween practical joke on a couple in our neighborhood. Their names were Barney and Blanche DeKuyper. Barney was a minister and Blanche was his wife. There was no particular reason why we chose to play the joke on them other than the fact that they weren't home at the time. A few nights before Halloween, Greg and I went and swiped a few jack o lanterns off of porches in the neighborhood. To fulfill our practical joke, we planned to display those jack o lanterns on top of someone's house. Since the DeKuyper's weren't home we chose their house. The only problem with that was they had a big black dog that would bite. Whenever they were gone, they would always leave the dog inside their house. So, on this particular night they were gone, and we knew the dog was inside, so this was the perfect time to execute our practical joke. We snuck over there in the dark carrying a 6ft ladder and 4 stolen jack o lanterns. We quietly climbed the fence and then we noticed that our ladder wasn't tall enough to help us to get on the roof. Then we noticed that the DeKuyper's had a picnic table in their back yard. We moved that table over close to the house and then we put the ladder on top of that picnic table. Obviously, safety was of no concern.

Greg climbed on top of the table and then up the ladder to the roof. I then handed him a couple of the jack o lanterns and some rope to tie them down. He walked to the highest point of the roof to start lining the pumpkins up. All at once, we saw the headlights of a car coming down the street. Greg laid face down on the roof so as not to be seen. The car pulled into the Hargraves driveway across the street. Someone got out of the car and went in. As soon as the coast was clear, we got busy again. I handed Greg one more jack o lantern and he carried it over and set it next to the others and tied them all down. At that point, I knew we had three down and one to go. All of a sudden, another car comes down the street only this time it pulls into the DeKuyper's driveway. It was Barney and Blanche and they were HOME! After they got out of the car and walked into their house I yelled to Greg, "Get off the roof! Their home! Hurry up!" Greg came running full speed across that roof making a ton of noise. We both knew they would let that crazy man-eating dog out at any second, so we had to get down grab the ladder and get over the fence as fast as possible. We could hear the dog barking inside the house, Greg was finally off the roof. We jumped off of the picnic table, grabbed the ladder and made a mad dash to the fence. By this time, we were no longer concerned with being quiet. With one quick motion we just threw the ladder over the fence. We could hear the sound of the dog barking getting louder. The back door suddenly opened as we were climbing the fence. Just as my feet landed on the ground on the other side of the fence, the DeKuyper's angry dog came raging across the yard toward the fence. Thankfully, by then we were safely on the other side. With the dog barking wildly and my heart nearly pounding out of my chest, we grabbed that ladder and ran away as fast as we could.

As it turned out, we were unable to finish our Halloween practical joke. Somehow the fear of getting eaten alive outweighed any desire to finish the job. We did end up getting 3 of the 4 jack o lanterns on the DeKuyper's roof. The funny thing was that they never bothered to get them down. The pumpkins literally stayed on that roof until they rotted away. The only thing that remained was the rope that we tied them down with. As mischievous teenagers, we spent a lot of time entertaining ourselves...sometimes at the expense of other people. We weren't violent or mean spirited. It was just silly mischief. Barney and Blanche just happened to be in the path of it. Hey, that's just the price you paid for living in the suburbs in the 1970's. You could fall prey to the Great Pumpkin Caper.

Lights, Camera, Action!

When I was little, my friends and I really enjoyed watching old black and white comedy teams like Abbott and Costello, Laurel and Hardy, The Three Stooges and my personal favorite The Marx Brothers. We would even pretend to be these characters. My friend Jack

and I had a collection of 200 ft. silent, black & white movies. Some of them were classic Marx Brothers and Abbott and Costello movies and some were old monster movies like Frankenstein and Godzilla. We started out watching them on an old hand cranked movie editor but, I finally got a projector for Christmas. Then, we could watch them on the wall. I loved watching those things. When I was little, there was something magical about turning a bare wall into a movie screen. This was obviously years before VCR's and DVD players.

Then, a couple of years later we unearthed an old super 8 movie camera that belonged to my friend Chris Logan's parents. We thought, "WOW! We could make our own movies!" Making movies would allow us the freedom to use our imagination to be as artistically terrible as teenage boys can be. And of course, we thought they would be "Awesome!"

We started out staying close to our comedic roots. That meant a "Mack Sennett pie in the face, slapstick kind of film". Our first 5-minute movie was filmed by my brother Jerry. My friend Chris Logan and I starred in it. It was filmed in my basement. Keeping with the slapstick tradition, there was a lot of slapping, knocking and even a pie in the face for good measure. For our next movie, we wanted it to look more like an old silent movie, so we ordered some black & white film from the new drug store down the street. This 8-minute movie was titled "Beans, Chops and Kops". Jerry played the role of Ford Sterling, the police chief of the Keystone Cops. We even edited in some footage of the real Keystone Cops into our movie. So much for copyright infringement. ;-) I played the role of silent movie legend Fatty Arbuckle in the film. Right as we began shooting this movie the light burned out on our camera. That meant that most of the film was shot too dark to see very clearly, which was kind, of sad because looking back, I would say it was our best movie. Most of them were terrible so that might not be saying much. "Beans, Chops and Kops was filmed during the winter of 1977.

Our next movie was titled "To Kill A Cop". It was filmed during the summer of 1978. It was a corny movie about what looked like a gang of white elementary kids that attack a cop and then pay the price for it. Several kids from the neighborhood played in the film. Me, Jerry, Chris, Greg, Gary, Archie and a few others were all in the movie.

For a short time, as teenage boys we really got into cheesy, B rated horror movies. Watching those awful movies greatly influenced some of our own movies. We made some horror movies as well. Of course, they were full of a lot of gratuitous violence and plenty of blood and gore. Our most gory movie was titled "Blood Bath". It was a movie about a vigilante, that was dedicated to hunting down and killing the man that murdered his uncle. Chris, Greg, Kurt, myself and a few other kids were all in that movie. We made a few other terrible horror movies as well. There was "Madhouse" and "Possessed" just to name a couple. We would always use Heinz ketchup as blood. Back then, we went through several bottles of ketchup. Why teenage boys enjoy gory horror movies is a mystery to me.

After that, we thought we would try a claymation movie. It's a method of animation in which clay figures are filmed using stop-motion photography. My friend Randy and I had a passion for old vintage rock & roll performances. There was no performance bigger than Woodstock. So, we made a miniature figure of the legendary guitarist Jimi Hendrix and his band out of clay. They were about 5 inches tall. Randy made a miniature Stratocaster guitar to put on our small clay Hendrix. Then, we made the other 2 members of the band (Noel Redding & Mitch

Mitchell) out of clay as well. Randy made a small bass guitar to go on Noel Redding. Then, he made a tiny drum set out of cardboard for the clay drummer Mitch Mitchell. We built a miniature set of the Woodstock stage. We tried our hand at stop motion animation. We would film a little bit and stop, then we would move our clay rock stars and film a little more. It was very time consuming so in the end, we only filmed about 2 minutes of it. After all that work, I wish we had been more patient and filmed it longer. It would have been neat if we had saved that clay Jimi Hendrix. I'm sure we destroyed it. We could be destructive little monsters.

The only other claymation type of movie we made was our spoof of Mr. Bill from the legendary Saturday Night Live show. The real Mr. Bill was made out of clay and got its start on Saturday Night Live as a Super 8 film sent in response to the show's request for home movies during the first season. Randy and I thought it would be fun to make our clay Mr. Bill. We made two short Mr. Bill films. One we simply titled "The Mr. Bill Show" and the other one was titled "Mr. Bill In Space". They were silly and fun to make.

I grew up during the 1960's and 70's. As a lot of boys did back then, we glamorized the old gangsters from the 1930's like John Dillinger, Pretty Boy Floyd, Baby Face Nelson and Bonnie and Clyde. So, we even made our own gangster movie. It was about a fictional bank robber named Rocky Malone. The movie was called "Rocky's Gang". I played the lead role of Rocky Malone and Chris played the role of G-man Melvin Purvis. The film was what you would expect of your typical gangster movie with lots of gunfire and bloodshed. Greg, Chris, Todd, myself and a couple others all starred in that movie.

Our love of classic comedy teams popped again as we parodied The Three Stooges. Obviously, being uncreative we called our version "The Three Stupid's". Before making this one, we collected aluminum cans and newspapers to be recycled for money. Then, we bought all the eggs and cool whip that our money would buy. We planned to return to our slapstick roots and make an over the top pie fight movie. Oddly enough, we filmed this pie fighting extravaganza on a neighbor's patio as they stood at their kitchen window and watched us in total disbelief. To my memory, that poor elderly couple were literally speechless after watching us kids make such a colossal mess of their patio! Me, Chris and a couple of other kids all starred in that movie.

After growing up watching Abbott And Costello, we came up with our own comedy team. We created Harry And Oliver. I played Harry and Chris played Oliver. We made 2 movies as these characters. The first one was titled The Haunted House". It was just a silly movie about two guys that spend the night in a haunted house. Our other Harry And Oliver movie was titled "Here's to the Army". It was about two guys that are drafted into the Army. Both movies were highly influenced by Abbott And Costello and they were a little raunchy but fun to make.

During our early teenage years, these were some of the things we enjoyed doing. I know it seems rather corny now, but we spent a considerable amount of time just planning and making these silly movies. We used our imagination and our simple creativity to come up with new ideas of things to do. This was decades before the internet, gaming and smart phones. We didn't sit around on a phone. Among many other things, we rode our bikes, ran through the woods, camped out, rode skateboards, ran the streets of our neighborhood and we made movies.

At the time, I think we must have been pretty unique compared to other kids I knew at school. No other kids I knew at school were making movies with their friends in their neighborhood. It gave us something interesting to do and it kept us out of trouble. Doing unusual things like making movies with my friends was just another thing that helped my childhood to be as full and rich as it was. In our movies I got to become a silent movie star, part of a comedy team, a director, a rock star and a gangster from the 1930's. All that before I was even 18 years old. Looking back, I know now that I had an awesome childhood. Heck, I even have the film to prove it.

Not just a Disaster at Sea

This should go without saying but, what a teenager deems as a "great idea" doesn't always turn out to be such a "great idea". Obviously, that is an understatement. All that being said, as teenagers, we got this "GREAT IDEA" of making a shipwreck movie. We had watched the movie, "A Night to Remember". It was a movie about the Titanic. Instead of making one about the Titanic, we decided to make our own shipwreck movie titled "Disaster at Sea". It was about a fictional ship called "The Britannica" that was capsized after it struck aN oil barge. It would turn out to be our last movie. By this time, we had started making our movies under our own film studio called Alantic Pictures Inc.

Again, Randy was the force behind the creative design of our film. If you know anything about old science fiction then, Randy was the "Ray "Harryhausen" of our neighborhood. He could make just about anything by hand. This time, Randy built a miniature passenger ship complete with all the aesthetic detail to make it look as authentic as possible. He then built a small oil barge to the same scale as the ship. It took a few weeks as we stayed busy planning out the movie and Randy finished up the important movie props.

Overall, this would go down as our most ambitious film to date. Making a movie about a disaster at sea when we didn't even have a large body of water to film it in, would prove to be very challenging. We first thought we would put our ship in a big washtub to film the water scenes but, it wasn't big enough. I decided to ask my sister Patricia if we could use my nephew Demian's wading pool, to film our water scenes. She gave us permission to use the wading pool. When I asked her if we could use it, I left out one small detail. We planned to catch our ship on fire and burn it up. (While still in the wading pool of course.)

After we finished our planning and prep work, we finally started filming our movie. I played the captain of the ship. Even though the movie was filmed with a silent movie camera, we had planned to put sound to it at a later date. After we filmed most of our indoor scenes it was time to film the ship colliding with the oil barge. We had put a couple of small medicine bottles filled with gas in the hull of the ship. Our plan was that when the two collided there would be a small explosion. Well, we kept trying to get the ship to ignite while filming. We weren't having much luck, so we went to get the gas can. That was a bad idea. Determined to get a "small" explosion, Jerry doused gas on the ship. Things went from calm to out of control in seconds. All at once, a small spark on the ship ignited an explosion that blew flames across the pool. For a few seconds, it looked as though the whole pool of water was on fire. Suddenly, flames went from the pool up to the gas can that Jerry was holding. With one motion, Jerry threw the gas can across the yard as fire followed it spewing flames across the yard. With flames still going in the pool, Jerry started stomping around in the wading pool trying to get the fire out. My other friends were stomping around out in the yard trying to put that fire out. All of this took place in a matter of a few seconds. Water can definitely burn when mixed with gas. A lesson learned. I guess you could say my short acting career ended with a BANG!

By the time the fire was out, and the smoke cleared, the wading pool had been burned and stomped flat. There were burned patches of grass in the yard from the flaming gas can that had been slung across the yard. My friends were suddenly remembering they had things to do at home and had to leave, kind of like on "Leave It to Beaver" when Eddie Haskell and Larry Mondello leave Wally and the Beaver holding the bag when things went wrong. I can't say I blame them for bolting. My dad could be very intimidating after he got mad so most of my friends wanted nothing to do with him. As to be expected, Patricia was pretty upset that we destroyed Demian's wading pool and my dad was furious about us doing something so dangerous and for the burnt places in the yard. Funny how I can remember the reckless events of making that goofy movie, but I have no memory what the punishment was for doing something so dangerous. More than likely I was grounded. I guess the old saying is true. Kids do the darnedest things!

What's on the Idiot Box?

Growing up in the 1970's was a lot of fun. Back then, kids breakfast cereal had a prize in the box. Inside almost every box of cereal was a game, a cardboard record to play, or a random toy that brought joy from the breakfast table straight to your hands. If you were a patient kid, you'd keep eating cereal until the plastic wrapped toy fell into your bowl. If you were like I was, you stuck your hand deep into the box as soon as you opened it, and immediately fished out the prize. As a kid, I would wake up early and grab a bowl of Captain Crunch, Honeycomb, Sugar Smacks or Rice Krispies cereal and then sit down and enjoy my favorite Saturday morning cartoons. I watched "Scooby Doo", "The Jetsons" and "Fat Albert'. But, my favorite by far was "The Bugs Bunny, Road Runner Hour". That was some great stuff!

I can also remember watching TV in the afternoon when I got home from school. Back then, there were only 4 TV stations. We always seemed to have plenty of things to watch. In the early days of WDRB, they showed great afternoon programs for kids. It would start at 3:00pm with Presto the Clown. He performed magic tricks, sent out birthday greetings to children and chatted with puppets Honey Bunny and J. Fred Frog. He would also introduce great cartoons from, "Yogi Bear", "Quick Draw McGraw" to "Tom and Jerry" and magic tricks all in the same show. It was a kid's dream come true. The afternoon line up was Ultraman, Speed Racer, The Three Stooges, Batman, Spiderman, Gilligan's Island, Hogan's Heroes, The Munster's and many more. My favorite after school show was "Leave It to Beaver". Every episode Beaver would always stumble from one childhood mishap to another. The show had a wonderful moral component to it.

At night we would watch "Happy Days". It was a fun sitcom about a suburban Milwaukee family that was coming of age during the 1950's. As a young boy, I thought Fonzie was very cool. My mother's favorite show back then was probably "The Mary Tyler Moore Show". That show was about a perky, thirty-something career woman named Mary Richards who settles in Minneapolis after breaking up with her boyfriend. My mom loved that show, probably because it depicted a strong independent woman. To this day, the opening theme song to that show is without question the most uplifting and positive of any show on television.

We would also watch Sanford And Son, Mash, The Andy Griffith Show, The Walton's and my favorite, All in The Family. We all loved All in the Family. I once told my mom that Archie reminded me of my dad. My mom was highly offended by that. Gee, I can't imagine why. ;-)

On Sunday mornings my sister, (Patti Sue) would watch "Star Trek" and then we would always watch the Abbott & Costello film festival that came on every Sunday. We loved Bud and Lou. Sunday night we would always watch Mutual of Omaha's Wild Kingdom and then we would watch The Wonderful World of Disney.

During the winter of 1977, we sat down as a family and watched the epic miniseries "Roots". The 12-hour television event was about a slave named Kunta Kinte and his family's battle to break free. It was based on Alex Haley's book of the same name. The miniseries became landmark television to say the least. The subsequent audience ratings were unprecedented: 85% of television households, or 130 to 140 million Americans (more than half the U.S. population) saw at least part of the series. An estimated 100 million viewers tuned in for the two-hour finale on Sunday, January 30, 1977. The miniseries was on for eight consecutive nights and we tuned in every night. When I was growing up, my mom watched all the historical events that came on TV. She watched the moon landing, all the Watergate hearings, every presidential debate, the Summer and Winter Olympics, presidential inaugurations, Princess Diana's wedding and her funeral and the horrible events of 9/11.

We watched lots of sports on TV as well. I was a big Minnesota Vikings fan. My mom really got into pro football too. Mom had 2 favorite teams. In the early 70's her favorite team was the Miami Dolphins and in the mid

70's she cheered for the Oakland Raiders. She would scream at the TV over bad penalties and literally get up and jump up and down in total elation when her team scored a touchdown. My mom and I were both big Louisville Cardinal fans. Watching the first real dream game in 1983 on TV was an incredible thing to see. The dream game was on March 26, 1983, in Knoxville, Tennessee, in the Mideast Regional final, with a trip to the Final Four on the line. That was the game that made me a huge Louisville fan. I loved the Cardinals high energy style of play. Guards Lancaster Gordon and Milt Wagner gave Louisville one of the best backcourts in America. With Charles Jones at center and Rodney and Scooter McCray at forward, the Cardinals had an unstoppable full court press. That team was outstanding. Three years later the Cards would win the national championship. The 1986 championship season was awesome. My mom and I watched live games on TV or we would stay up late and watch a delayed broadcast of the game after the local news. My dad hated basketball but, he loved football. My dad was born in Tennessee and he was a big Tennessee Volunteers fan. I would sit with my dad and watch the Big Orange play on TV. I too became a Volunteers fan. My dad and I would also watch Monday Night Football together every week. Dad and I also enjoyed watching boxing. Our favorite fighter back then was Iron Mike Tyson because he was a no-nonsense heavyweight fighter that ended nearly every match with a knockout.

I would watch everything from Wide World of Sports, Battle of the Network Stars, all the Super Bowls, the Big Red Machine, Muhammad Ali fights to Evel Knievel jumps. I watched it all on just 4 TV channels. Now, most households have cable or satellite TV with more than a hundred channels to watch. There is way more stuff on, but far less stuff worth watching. Sadly, with all those channels, you are mostly left with reality TV trash. When there were fewer channels, it meant you had to really have talent to even get on a show. That made for much more artistic, thought provoking television.

I grew up in front of the TV. The first color television set we ever had my dad won from a filling station raffle. It only had a 13" screen, but it was in color and we were thrilled to have it. Life seemed much simpler and more innocent back then and so were the TV shows. The 1970's was a wonderful time to grow up. As a kid, Mr. Rogers assured us it was "a wonderful day in the neighborhood." and J.J. from "Good Times" told us everything was "DYNAMITE"! When you're a kid, that is an awesome thing to be told. Even if the person telling you that is coming to you through the Idiot Box.

Thanksgiving Memories

Looking back at what Thanksgiving Day was like when I was a kid, many thoughts come to mind. I remember waking up to the smell of food filling the house and the sounds of Mom working in the kitchen preparing a Thanksgiving meal for her family. Whenever I was very little, I remember Biff and Patti Sue watching the Thanksgiving Day parade on TV. Mom would always set the table with her nice silverware and the China that my dad sent her when he was in the Army. She would use her nice tablecloth and napkins as well. In general, Mom did not enjoy cooking much so everything she cooked was pretty basic and simple, but it was good. I always really enjoyed my mom's stuffing on thanksgiving. There was nothing special about how she made it but it was special to me. She would always fix a traditional Thanksgiving meal complete with turkey, stuffing, gravy, sweet potatoes, green beans, deviled eggs, mashed potatoes, cranberry sauce and dinner rolls. Dad would always carve the turkey. After the meal, Mom would serve pumpkin pie or pecan pie for dessert.

As the years went on and Patti Sue, Biff and Jerry moved out, they would come back for our family Thanksgiving meal. When Patti Sue and Roger still lived in the trailer, she would always bring something homemade and it was delicious. Our Thanksgiving meals varied over the years from small gatherings to large gatherings. Mom, Daddy, Patti Sue, Roger, Demian, Deidre, Biff, Sondra, Cami, Kaycee, Jerry, Diana, Chantel, Aunt Rema, Aunt Bessie, Aunt Rose, Uncle Dukie, Doyle and Hal have all sat at our Thanksgiving table at some point over the years.

After the big meal, everyone would sit around and talk or retire to the living room to watch pro football. Thanksgiving Day usually meant you suffered through watching the Detroit Lions get the crap beat out of them by just about any other team in the league. For more than 60 years the Lions played every Thanksgiving Day. I'm sure most of those games they lost because for many, many years the Lions have been one of the worst teams in football. The only thing remotely interesting about watching the Detroit Lions was to watch Barry Sanders. To me, he was the greatest running back in the history of football. Sadly, for him, he was just on a bad team.

Since my mom's passing back in 2008 there has not been another Thanksgiving gathering at my house on Riverview Lane. I am totally at peace with that. All good things must come to an end. For a few years now, we have started a new Thanksgiving tradition. My wife (Sherri) and I go to Jerry and Denise's house for a nice, relaxing Thanksgiving dinner. It's a wonderful meal complete with plenty of southern comfort and warm conversation.

As a little kid, I remember back in elementary school learning about Thanksgiving. It was all about the pilgrims, the Indians and the Mayflower. There were always turkey decorations hanging up in the classrooms. They taught you all about the importance of being thankful on a holiday called Thanksgiving. After you get older and you suffer some heartache, sickness and loss, you learn the real meaning of being thankful in your own life. You learn that life is very fragile, and nothing is certain. Nowadays, I'm a man in my 50's and I've lived through a few things. I have a lot to be thankful for. I'm thankful for my siblings and how much they mean to me. I'm thankful for my health. It's something to never take for granted. I'm thankful for my friends. They bring me support, joy and laughter. The one's that have stuck by me are worth far more than money can buy. I'm thankful for having a bad back. It teaches me fortitude through adversity. I'm thankful for Tom the cat. He is full of love and loyalty. I'm thankful for having cerebral palsy. It has taught me perseverance and patience. I am thankful for the parents I had. They made me the man I am today. I'm thankful for my wife. I waited for her for most of my life. She was definitely worth the long wait. I am also very thankful to know Jesus Christ as my Lord and Savior.

Yes, Thanksgiving is about far more than just pilgrims, turkey dinners and football. It's about spending time with family and friends. But, it's mostly about being thankful for the many blessings we have. With all the negativity in this world, Thanksgiving is a wonderful time to focus on a lifetime of blessings.

Aunts, Uncles and Cousins

The older I get the more I notice just how many things have changed since I was a kid. Some of those changes have been somewhat gradual and subtle over time but they are changes none the less. When I was little, all children were raised to address their parents' brothers and sisters with the title of Aunt or Uncle. We weren't allowed to call them by just their first names. I'm sure we were taught to do that out of respect. In other words, my mom had a sister named Rose. We were all raised to address Rose as Aunt Rose. It would have been disrespectful for us kids to address her any other way. I think there is something lost in how we communicate when we do away with these types of traditions. It is with that in mind that I wish to pay my aunts and uncles the respect they deserve.

When I was little, I had a few aunt's and uncle's that were very special to me. This story tells just a little bit about those special people. My dad's family all lived in Tennessee and Georgia. My mom's family all lived in rural Kentucky where she came from. This story is dedicated to those few aunts and uncles that meant the most to me.

My Aunt Wilma was my dad's sister and my Uncle Harry was Aunt Wilma's husband. They lived right next to my grandmother in Rossville Georgia. It was always a blast to visit Aunt Wilma and Uncle Harry. Aunt Wilma always spoiled us kids by fixing us all of our favorite things to eat. She would always have Brown Cow ice cream bars and ice cream sandwiches for us. Aunt Wilma was a wonderful cook and she would always have a cake baked as well, usually a coconut cake or a German chocolate cake.

On Mom's side of the family there are a few aunts and uncles as well. My mom was very close to her Aunt Bessie and Uncle Arthur. My parents would go to visit them each- and-every Sunday. As kids, we were expected to go with them. Aunt Bessie was my mom's Mothers sister. My mom's Mother passed away before I was born, so sadly, I never got to meet her. My mom was close to her Mother and it would have been a treat to have gotten to know her. I guess after Mom lost her mother, she began to get close to Aunt Bessie. Compared to where we lived, Aunt Bessie and Uncle Arthur lived out in the country. They had a nice place. Uncle Arthur always whitewashed their trees. Jerry and I would wander around outside investigating things. They had a pretty fenced in yard that also included a small pond. Next to the pond there was a small statue of a black man fishing. Their yard also included a gazing ball and an old sundial. They had an outhouse that always smelled of lime. It was fun to go and visit them, plus most of the time when we went to visit them, we also got to go to Bernheim Forest and feed the ducks. That was always fun.

My mom had two sisters. Aunt Rose was her older sister and Aunt Ruby was her younger sister. Aunt Ruby was married to my Uncle Willy. He was friendly to us kids but, he was a rather loud and braggadocious man. Aunt Ruby was friendly to us as well. They moved around a lot. They finally moved themselves and their five girls away from the rest of the family and were gone for a while before Aunt Rose insisted that her husband (my Uncle Dukie) and my dad hunt them down so she could tell them that Grandpa Thornton was sick. I think at the time; they were living on some farm in eastern Kentucky. They never lived anywhere long. They were always on the run.

Aunt Rose was Mom's dearest sister and her life-long best friend. They were very close. Aunt Rose was a few years older than my mom. They had a lot of the same interests and they were very similar in nature. Her husband's name was Delmar but, everyone called him Dukie. All of us kids called him Uncle Dukie. He was a good man and we all loved him. He had a fun, jovial personality. When Jerry and I were kids, we were in the Cub Scouts and Mom was our den mother. Back then, Uncle Dukie made our pinewood derby car for the annual Cub Scouts Pinewood Derby. I thought that was cool. As a kid, I also thought it was cool that Uncle Dukie liked to watch the classic Peanuts cartoons. Even nowadays as an adult, I enjoy the old Charlie Brown cartoons as well. Sadly, Uncle Dukie would suddenly die from a massive heart attack at the age of 47. He was a good man who would be greatly missed.

Aunt Rose and Uncle Dukie had two sons. Paul and Mark. Paul was an athletic kid. He played high school football. As a young man, Paul would get married and father two children. Sadly, after that Paul was drafted and was sent to the war in Vietnam, where he lost his legs. The only memories I have of Paul are of him in a wheelchair. Tragically, shortly after he came back home, he was killed in a car accident. Mark would grow up and get married and then father a daughter. He would go on to become a preacher. I used to enjoy hearing Mark tell stories about Grandma Thornton. He was a good storyteller.

Years after Uncle Dukie died, Aunt Rose married a man by the name of Doyle Wentworth. By this time, all of us kids were grown so none of us ever got close to Doyle. He and Aunt Rose were married for a few years until Doyle was killed in a car wreck. My Aunt Rose is a strong woman that has lived through a lot of tragedy. During all her tragedies, Mom stayed by her side to offer love and support. My dad was very close to Aunt Rose as well. He looked after her and helped her out with things after Uncle Dukie and Doyle passed away.

Shortly after Aunt Rose retired from Jim Beam Distillery, she met a wonderful man by the name of Hal Case. He had recently retired from the railroad. By then, they each had their own homes and they were both financially secure. I'm pretty sure my Aunt Rose and Hal decided early on that they wanted to keep their independence, so they agreed to not get married. Even though Hal and Aunt Rose never got married, they have lived like a couple for many, many years. They go everywhere together and spent most of their time together. It's just that they each continue to live in their own homes. Mom and Dad both thought the world of Hal. He is a friendly gentleman that has a very laid-back nature about him. Hal always enjoys telling stories to anyone that was willing to listen. Over time it was clear that Hal has become part of our family. He was always there

to help out in any way he could during both of my parents' illnesses and
subsequent passing's.

My mom had three brothers but two of them died at birth or shortly afterward. Billy Eugene and Micheal Tracy were the two that died. My Uncle Carl was the only one of her brothers we knew because he was the only one that lived. His given name is Thomas, but everyone calls him Carl. To all of us kids, he was Uncle Carl. I was named after Uncle Carl. We both share the same middle name, "Ray". Even though I am the one that was named after Uncle Carl, my brother Jerry is the one that has his mannerisms. Mom use to say that Jerry is a lot like Uncle Carl. Jerry and Uncle Carl even walk alike. Uncle Carl is married to my Aunt Dorothy. Uncle Carl and Aunt Dorothy have 3 kids. Loretta, Marion and Roxanne. When we were kids, I remember my sister Patti Sue always enjoyed going to visit Uncle Carl because Aunt Dorothy always had some little critters that she was taking care of like a stray dog or a cat. She might be leaving out food for a rabbit, a raccoon or some other critter that might need some help. All of us kids loved Aunt Dorothy because she had a bigger than life childlike personality. She also has a very caring heart. I think that is where her drive to take care of the animals came from. Uncle Carl is a hardworking man that was very dedicated to providing for his family. He worked at Jim Beam distillery for 45 years before he retired. For more then 50 years, Uncle Carl also took care of the Vine Hill Cemetery in Clermont Ky. Along with keeping the grass mowed and trimmed on a weekly basis, he would do lots of detail work as well. Every year in the days leading up to Memorial Day weekend, Uncle Carl would meticulously go through and clean all of the headstones in the cemetery. His care of that little country cemetery was without question, a labor of love and it showed. When I was little, we would go to that cemetery every Memorial Day and spend the whole afternoon visiting with my other aunts, uncles and cousins. That always seemed to be a joyous occasion. It was almost like a family reunion. My Uncle Carl always took great pride in that old cemetery. He is a born-again believer and he was chairman of the deacons at Clermont Baptist Church for many years. Uncle Carl is also a very strong southern democrat. As I got older, I grew to appreciate him more and more. I always enjoy a high-spirited political conversation with him.

I have a great deal of respect and appreciation for my Uncle Carl. He is a lead by example kind of guy. He stands up for what he believes in. Uncle Carl epitomizes integrity and hard work.

While going to church at Clermont during the 1980's I began to get close to my cousins Loretta and Marion. Loretta has a lot of her mother's characteristics and mannerisms. She is very dedicated to her family and her faith. We ran around a lot together back then and we participated in a lot of church activities together. Those are some special times in my life. Back then, I even sat with my cousin Marion and her husband all day while Marion was in labor waiting for her son to be born. Marion and I were very close. Years later, as my mom began her long battle with dementia, it was my cousin Marion that would step up to lend a hand right when we needed some extra help with Mom. I will forever be grateful to Marion for that. Even though because of our busy lives we don't talk much these days, Marion will always feel like a second sister to me.

Having extended family as you grow up is a pretty important thing. Just having a positive support system is a blessing. My aunts, uncles and cousins offered love and support at different stages of my life when I needed it most. I believe God puts different people in our path during our lives to guide us and help us along the way. Some of those people were my aunt's, uncle's and some were my cousins too. I loved them all.

Pets of all Kinds

I don't really consider myself an animal person but, as a kid, I sure had an interest in animals. My interest in animals goes way back to my early childhood. You could say it started when I was just one year old. On my first birthday, my mom and dad gave me a little female dachshund named Hilda. I couldn't say Hilda, so I called her Hootie. In time, the whole family was calling her Hootie as well. She was a great dog. Even though she was just given to me, Hootie was without question, a dog for the whole family. She loved to sit up on her butt with her front legs up in the air and beg for a treat. She was feisty and fun and always barked anytime someone knocked at the door. We would take her on trips with us. Anytime my mom would get the suitcases out, Hootie would get all excited because she loved to go on trips with us. For 16 years, she was part of our house and part of our family. After she got old and started having a host of health issues, we finally had to put Hootie to sleep. At the time, I was only 16 years old and that was the first time I had ever felt profound loss. She was a wonderful pet and after she died, we never had another dog. She was the best and it's pointless to try to replace the best.

Whenever I was a very small boy, I was just crazy about little animals and bugs. I was so amazed by insects that Mom even got Jerry and I a bug catcher. After a short time, the bug catcher broke. After that, we punched a few holes, with a nail, into the lid of a mayonnaise jar, and used that to catch our bugs. I was into it more than Jerry was. I guess you could say, I was a bug crazy boy. Ha! I would run around catching everything from butterflies, honeybees, grasshoppers, katydids to praying mantises and lightening bugs. Once, in a while we would also catch a June bug and tie a string around its leg and then hold on to the string while the June bug buzzed all around us. To me, these were some of the simple pleasures of summertime.

Then I discovered frogs, terrapins, lizards, snakes and crawdads. As a boy, I was the most interested in tadpoles, frogs and turtles. It was always fun to catch some tadpoles and put them in a fishbowl and feed them fish food for a few days and watch them slowly turn into frogs. Catching a green snake in the wooded graveyard behind our house was always fun to do as well. I would sometimes catch a terrapin and put it in a box and feed it for a couple of days and then turn it loose. Nowadays most of my neighbors want the perfect weed free yard, so they have their yards sprayed with all these pesticides to kill the weeds, but it kills all the bugs, terrapins and toad frogs as well. Sadly, now it has been years since I have seen a toad frog anywhere near my house. Because of that, now most little boys grow up and they never even get to see a honeybee, a terrapin or a frog in person. They are growing up without seeing the wonder of nature. They have no idea what they are missing. When I was a boy, I was playing with bugs, frogs, terrapins and snakes. Today, boys sit around and play video games.

I was so into terrapins that Mom even bought Jerry and I a couple of red-eared slider turtles from the pet shop. They were little green turtles. Those particular breed of turtles were later banned from the United States because they shed salmonella and made a lot of people very sick. We didn't have ours very long anyway until they died. Mom later bought Jerry an aquarium for his birthday. It was displayed in the kitchen. The aquarium was filled with guppies, Tetras and an Angelfish. It was also interesting and fun to have around.

When my sister Patricia and her husband Roger came back from Germany, they brought two cats back with them. Their names were Sybil and Sasha. My dad hated those cats with a passion. He was clearly not an animal person. Jerry and I would later have a parakeet but while we were asleep one night, Sybil came into our room and got the parakeet out of the cage and ate it. Obviously, it's not a good idea to own a bird and a cat at the same time.

As a kid, I developed a fascination with hamsters and gerbils. When I was in the 5th grade, my teacher had a hamster cage in his classroom. Even though I hated school, I looked forward to going to his class everyday just to see those hamsters. As a teenager I had a male hamster I named McVicar. I named him after John McVicar. He was a convicted armed robber who escaped from prison. I named the hamster McVicar because he was always escaping from his cage. He was so noisy that every night I would put his cage in the living room so I could sleep. Early one morning before daylight, I was awoken by my dad saying, "Jimi, that damn hamster is loose in the living room!" I knew right away that McVicar had escaped again and I better get up and find him.

Years and years later in February of 2010, I bought my wife (Sherri) a hamster that she hand-picked herself. We named the little long-haired teddy bear hamster Bernie after Bernheim Forest because that is where we went on our first date. Even though I had owned a few other hamsters while growing up, none of them were like Bernie. From the day we got him, he never bit anyone. He was completely white, and he kept a very clean cage. Sherri was crazy about him. Bernie brought lots of joy and laughter for about 2 and a half years. He was the perfect hamster. He left behind a little lady hamster that lived across the room from him. Her name was Minnie Mae. She was a year younger than Bernie, but way busier. She was so busy that I nicknamed her "Manic Minnie". She spent most of her time climbing all over the top of her cage upside down. She was also very sneaky about finding ways to get out of her cage so she could run for freedom. After being caught from yet another routine escape, she always seemed happy to be safely put back in her cage. Almost as if she were a dog, Minnie would sit on the upper landing of her cage facing the door and wait for me to come home from work. She would be waiting for her nightly treat. Bernie and Minnie Mae were the first two pets that Sherri and I had together. Even though they were just hamsters, they were great pets and will never be forgotten.

The last part of this story is reserved for a cat named Thomas Edison Caudill but, we just call him Tom. He belonged to Sherri's son Drew. Now, Tom is by no means your average cat. You see, Tom only has 3 legs but, don't tell him that because he doesn't know it. He lost his leg in a freak accident. Years ago, when Drew was working at McDonalds, a co-worker rescued a littered of kittens that had been left along the side of the road. Tom had ventured away from the rest of the litter and had been hit by a car. After his co-worker had taken Tom to the vet for treatment, she brought him to Drew. After that, Tom lived with Drew for many years.

In the early spring of 2014 Drew took a new job in Denver Colorado. He had a big decision to make. Drew had first planned to take Tom to Denver with him. I had already been worrying about what a hard time that I knew Sherri would have when Drew moved away. Sherri has always been a big animal person and she has always loved Drew's cat. One evening, Drew called and said he really didn't think it would be a good idea to take Tom to Denver with him because he would be traveling so much with his new job. Drew asked her if we might consider taking Tom. I heard Sherri tell Drew on the phone, "I don't think Jimi would ever want to have a cat in the house but, I will ask him and let you know what he says." When she got off of the phone she came and told me the situation that Drew was in with his cat. Since I knew Sherri was going to miss Drew terribly when he moved, I decided to tell her that he could come and live with us if she wanted him. I could tell Sherri was shocked that I offered such a thing. It was obvious that Sherri really wanted Tom and Tom really needed a new home. So, that is how Tom came to live with us.

Tom has a lot of personality and it shows up a lot in his tail. Tom's tail never stops moving. I have a few nicknames for Tom. A couple of my pet names for him are "Mr. Floppy Tail" and "Tail Tappin Tom". Without question, he is a very social cat. He demands a lot of your time and loves a belly rub as much as Sherri loves chocolate. Because Tom only has 3 legs, most of the time he makes a thumping sound as he limps across the floor. Well, because I have cerebral palsy, I too thump around the house because of my limp. I told Sherri that now she must listen to two of us thumping around the house. Sherri says that since Tom lived with Drew for so many years that he had become a man's cat. I have never been a cat person but, for some reason Tom has taken a liking to me. Much of the time he follows me around like a dog would. He even acts like a dog sometimes. If you sit down in the living room, then most of the time Tom wants to come and get in your lap. Tom is a big part of the family. So, if you come to the Huckaby house to visit, you will also be visiting Tom as well. On a nice warm day, you will find Tail Tappin Tom sitting at the front door looking out just waiting for someone to entertain him. Just come right on in because he would love to get to know you and if you stop and rub his belly, he will be your friend forever. And for a pet owner, having a pet that's a friend forever is just about all you could ever hope for.

Christmas Anticipation

When I was a kid, Christmas time was an unbelievably special time of year. Looking back, one thing stands out, "Christmas Anticipation". For me, everything about Christmas was exciting, so I really looked forward to it. I looked forward to "all of it".

It first started with anticipating the arrival of the J.C. Penney Catalog. You see, in late fall the J.C. Penney Christmas Catalog would come in the mail and we would look through it and start our Christmas wish list. After a lot of careful consideration, we would finally pick out what we wanted our Aunt Wilma (my dad's sister) to get us for Christmas. So, we would cut the picture and description out of the catalog and mail it to my Aunt that lived in Rossville Georgia. Then, we would go there to visit in December, and we would get that exact gift from her. Even though we knew what it was, it was still always exciting.

Then there was all the anticipation of putting the Christmas tree up. Us kids would start begging Mom shortly after Thanksgiving to let us put up the tree. She would never let us put it up until about 2 weeks before Christmas. The first tree I can remember was a silver tree that had a color wheel with it. The color wheel had blue, green, orange and red on it that was supposed to change the color of the tree. It didn't really do that, but to a four-year-old boy like me, it was all shiny and sparkly and I thought it was neat. A year or two later we got a green artificial tree. I always wanted blinking colored lights on our tree, but Mom didn't let us have blinking lights because it gave her a headache. One Christmas season when I was about 5 years old, I was hospitalized with the croup. While I was in the hospital for a few days, my family decided to put up the Christmas tree. By the time I got out of the hospital and came home it was nearly

Christmas. Mom had saved a few ornaments just for me to put on the tree. That is one of my nicest and warmest memories.

For me, everything about Christmas was exciting. There was a lot of anticipation just leading up to the Christmas cartoons they showed every year. I made sure I was in front of the TV by 8pm to watch the cartoons on network TV. Watching those cartoons was something when we were kids. We used to wait all year long just for a 1/2-hour show. If we were lucky, they played a couple of them back to back, so you'd have a whole hour of fun. From "Frosty, The Snowman and "Rudolph The Red Nosed Reindeer" to "The Little Drummer Boy" and "How the Grinch Stole Christmas", those cartoons were must see TV for every kid. My personal favorite was "A Charlie Brown Christmas". It was a true Christmas classic.

Around Christmas time my sister Patti Sue would lay in the bed with Jerry and I and we would sing Christmas carols from an old songbook. I still have that songbook. That is a warm Christmas memory too.

When I was a kid, if you watched the 6:00 news on Christmas Eve you would see Santa Claus and his sleigh flying across the screen on the radar during the weather. Looking back, the graphics were very poor, and the technology was lame, but to a 4-year-old it was exciting stuff.

We had a fun family tradition every year of always opening one present each, on Christmas Eve. That meant there was always lots of anticipation leading up to Christmas Eve. For some reason, that became a big deal. Jerry and I would spend a considerable amount of time shaking every one of our presents as we tried to decide exactly which present to choose to open on Christmas Eve. And then Dad was always there teasing us while trying to find out what we had gotten him for Christmas. He would say things like, "I already know what you got me so why don't you just tell me what it is?" Mom would say, "Bill!! You leave those kids alone!" Then, he would laugh and say, "I'm not doing anything."

After we opened our ONE carefully handpicked present, we would play with it for a while and then it was off to bed. After all, the next day would be Christmas morning. One year, Jerry and I opened walkie talkies and had a blast with them until we went to bed. Another year, my Christmas Eve present was a small red, white and blue, handheld transistor radio. That night I buried my head under the covers and softly listened to that radio until I gently drifted off to sleep. When I was little, I remember my oldest brother Biff would be up and down all night long just waiting for Christmas morning. As kids, due to the anticipation and excitement none of us could sleep very well the night before Christmas.

The first Christmas present I can remember getting was a fisher price barn. Another year, Jerry got the Ants in The Pants game and I got the board game Mouse Trap. One year, I got Lincoln Logs and Jerry got Tinkertoys. We played with those for hours. Another year I got a G.I. Joe and the army jeep to go with him. One year I got some hand painted civil war soldiers and I still have them. Another year, Jerry and I got a train set. That was very exciting. When I was about 10, I got my first camera. I really enjoyed that. My favorite Christmas present ever was probably a super 8 movie projector. Then, I could actually watch my super 8 movies on the wall and that was very cool. Obviously, this was years before there were VCR's or DVD players to watch movies in your house.

After all the gifts were opened, we would all sit down for a big Christmas meal complete with turkey that my mom had cooked. It was always delicious, and a wonderful time was had by all. Back then, Christmas day was a very respected Christian holiday. It represented the birthdate of Jesus Christ which meant pretty much nothing was open. The roads were quiet, the stores were all closed. Most of the gas stations were even closed. It would be silent outside. The most you would see or hear was a couple taking a walk or some kids out in front of their house trying out their new bikes while the roads were empty.

I'm in my 50's now, and as you would imagine a lot has changed. Christmas is still a very special time of year for me. So much so that back on Christmas Eve of 2012 and while kneeling next to the Christmas tree, I asked Sherri to marry me. She said "yes" and that became my all-time favorite Christmas present.

Nowadays, I still love Christmas just as much as ever, but in a different way. I love the simplicity of Christmas. Sherri and I don't buy many gifts. Christmas isn't about Black Friday shopping or how much money you spend. Christmas is about enjoying the magic of the season. It's all about celebrating the birth of Jesus and the magic of the season. It's about putting the tree up with those you love. Sherri and I just try to keep it simple. We enjoy visiting friends and family and making homemade cookies to give them. We enjoy driving around at night to look at the Christmas lights. We love to listen to all those traditional Christmas carols all throughout the Christmas season. I love to set out the old antique nativity scenes to represent the true meaning of Christmas. We enjoy going to a Christmas Eve service at church. With all of that to look forward too, I still have plenty of Christmas anticipation every year.

Jerry and Jimi anticipating a big Christmas

If it's not a Merry Christmas, It's a Happy Mother's Day

When I was about 11 or 12 years old, my oldest brother Biff took Jerry and I Christmas shopping to buy a gift for Mom. At the time Biff was dating Annette and she went with us. Jerry and I only had a few dollars to spend and we had no idea what to buy Mom for Christmas. After we arrived, Biff told us to meet him in the front of the store at 8:00.

Then, he and Annette walked away hand in hand to do their own shopping. Obviously, leaving Jerry and I to Christmas shop for Mom alone was without question a bad idea.

So, Jerry and I set out to buy Mom something for Christmas. On the way looking for a gift for Mom we got sidetracked by the toy department. We noticed they had the Monopoly board game on sale. Well heck, we just couldn't pass that up. So, we grabbed it, but we still needed to buy something for Mom. For some unknown reason, we got this crazy idea to buy Mom a dress for Christmas. First of all, young boys picking out a dress for a woman is not likely to end well, but since there was no one around with any common sense to stop us, we went with our plan. That's right, bad judgment and all and with no rhyme or reason, we forged ahead. We would pick a dress and hold it up and wonder if Mom could wear it or not. After doing that a few times, we settled on one and went with it. As crazy as it sounds, when we met back up with Biff and Annette with a Monopoly game and a dress, there were no questions asked. I'm sure to him, he took us shopping, what we bought after we got there was of no concern to him. Hey, Jerry and I set out to get something for Mom and so to us, it was mission accomplished! Plus, as a bonus we got a Monopoly game. Obviously, a blind man can see where this is headed but, two young boys had no clue.

Come Christmas morning, Mom opened her present from Jerry and me. She took it out of the box and held it up with this puzzled look on her face. With proud enthusiasm I said, "What do you think, Mom?" She said, "Well, it's pretty" but she still looked rather bewildered. Then I said, "Is something wrong with it? Will it fit?" She said, "Well, it's for someone short and fat." Then, without hesitation Jerry blurted out, "Well, we thought you were short and fat!" Everyone laughed, including Mom. She never let on that our choice for a Christmas gift was totally ridiculous. More then likely, Mom was just proud we bought her something, but I'm sure she returned that dress first chance she got.

To this day, I won't even buy my wife a dress if she isn't there to try it on. As a man in my 50's, I still have no clue about dress sizes. Though I do know that it's never a good idea to tell any woman that she looks "short and fat".

On Mother's Day of the following year, Dad took Jerry and I to the PX to get Mom a gift. We got her a light blue pitcher. Mom loved it! Years later, I found that same pitcher in her china cabinet with the gift tag tucked away inside of it. I took that to mean that we made up for the "short and fat dress" that we bought her for Christmas. I guess, to be a Mom is to be tolerant of her kids because they may not always get her the most appropriate gift, but I guess if she has patience, she just might get a gift she actually likes once in a while.

Music for the Soul

All my life I have had an interest in music that grew into a passion. My mom even wrote in my baby book that when I was one year old, "I loved to hear the theme song on the AFN Sports program." From an early age music touched something deep inside of me. A musician friend once told me if I hadn't been born with cerebral palsy then I would more then likely Have become a musician. I'm not sure about that, but I certainly have music in my soul.

When I was a kid, my oldest brother Biff bought me an album by the bubblegum group The Ohio Express. The album had the hits "Yummy, Yummy, Yummy" and "Chewy, Chewy" on it. Bubblegum music was happy, upbeat music. Bubblegum music were songs like "Sugar Sugar" by The Archies and "Knock Three Times" by Tony Orlando and Dawn. It was very corny, but I was just a kid and I loved it. Silly songs like that were the beginning of my love of music. When I was very little, I remember WKLO radio playing daily in our house. Also, my sister Patty Sue and my older brother Biff had a collection of records that I would listen to whenever I had the chance. They had the old 45 records of "Nice To Be With You" by Gallery, "Elusive Butterfly" by Bob Lind, "Abraham, Martin And John" by Dion, "Atlantis" by Donavon, "A Hard Day's Night" and "Please, Please Me" by The Beatles, "I'm A Believer" and "Pleasant Valley Sunday" both by The Monkees, just to name a few. I wore those records out. My sister had the Simon & Garfunkel album "Bridge Over Troubled Water". That album is a real classic. My mom listened to the Kris Kristofferson album "Songs of Kristofferson" and I enjoyed that one as well. Biff had the cassette "Hot August Night" by Neil Diamond. When Biff was gone, I would go into his bedroom and turn his stereo up and listen to that cassette and play air guitar for hours. That album was electric, a pure masterpiece! I also remember when I discovered John Denver. I had his greatest hits album. His music came from nature. It was very genuine and heartfelt. To this day, he is still one of my favorites.

And then I discovered Elvis Presley! I remember my friend Greg and I walking up our street when a neighborhood girl rode by on her bike and said, "Hey, did you all hear that Elvis died?" At the time, I had no idea how big that news was in the entertainment world. I was 14 when Elvis died and that is when I first started listening to him. My friend Jack and I listened to him all the time for about a year. We even made an Elvis scrapbook. Then after that, we got into beach music. Biff had The Beach Boys album "Little Deuce Coup" and I would listen to it every chance I got. Then Jack and I really got into Jan & Dean. They sang about drag racing, girls and surfing. We listened to them exclusively during the summer of 1979. That was great summertime music! Late that year, Jack and I went to see Jan & Dean in concert at the Derby Dinner Playhouse. We had a great time.

Then I heard "Cheap Trick at Budokan" for the first time and I really liked them. It was hard pop with an edge. By this point, I was getting older and I liked more current pop music. My friend Randy and I really got into Cheap Trick. Then we discovered The Who. The "Who's Next" album was an outstanding rock & roll record. Randy and I went to the theatre to see The Who movie, "The Kids Are Alright". We were totally blown away by their live performance of "Won't Get Fooled Again". They were the most electrifying rock & roll band of their time. From 1969 to 1978 they were incredible. A few months later, we went to the Vogue theatre to see a midnight showing of that movie again. The audience was cheering at the screen as if they were at a real rock concert. That was fun!

Once Randy and I walked from my house to Taylor Drug store just to buy the AC/DC album "Back in Black". We were exhausted when we got home so we just laid on my bed and listened to it. That is a great memory. For a while, I got into heavy metal music. I enjoyed Black Sabbath, Deep Purple and Rainbow a lot but, my favorite was the Blizzard of Ozz band with Ozzy Osbourne. The first time I ever heard the song "Crazy Train", I was blown away. Randy Rhoads played guitar on Ozzy's first two albums. He mixed heavy metal with classical guitar. It was something totally unique. He showcased that style in the songs, "You Can't Kill Rock and

Roll", "Diary of A Madman" and "Tonight". Randy was truly a guitar virtuoso. On March 19, 1982, I was deeply saddened to hear that he had been killed in a plane crash. In my eyes, he was the best guitar player ever. He was way ahead of his time and he was taken from this world way too soon.

When I was in high school, I really got into "The Wall" album by Pink Floyd. "Comfortably Numb" is a brilliant song from that record. It has one of the most melodic guitar solos ever recorded. A true masterpiece.

As I grew older, my taste in music evolved. After I became a Christian, I began listening to Christian music. Amy Grant, Don Watson and Michael
W. Smith were some of my favorites.

Just to prove that some things never change, as I grew older, I continued to really enjoy TV show theme songs. Some of my favorites were the theme songs from WKRP In Cincinnati, Mash, Good Times, Cheers, All in The Family, Mary Tyler Moore, Bugs Bunny theme, The Walton's, Mission Impossible and many more. Heck, I even liked TV show themes of shows that I didn't care for. TV show themes like Laverne & Shirley, The Jefferson's, Dallas, Little House on The Prairie, The Addams Family, Welcome Back Kotter and Star Trek. I even enjoyed that old jingle from that 1971 Coke commercial called, "I'd Love to Teach the World to Sing". To me, that wasn't just a commercial, it was beautiful. I've also always been a big fan of traditional Christmas music as well. I think the old classics like White Christmas are the best!

I've always used music to fit the mood I was in. As a teenager, if I were sad, I would listen to sad songs. Sometimes, I would be in a country mood, other times I would be in a hard rock mood. Now as an adult, on Valentine's Day, I hand pick a group of songs to make my wife Sherri a CD. I use music to communicate my feelings in a deeper way to help Sherri understand how much I love her. There are no words to express just how much Sherri means to me but, music helps me to be able to convey all of my emotion for her into a feeling that she can hear. For me, that is what the true essence of music is all about. Music isn't something you can see or touch. Music is something you feel in your soul. That is why when The Beatles sang, "All You Need Is Love", everyone knew exactly what they meant. We all know "Love Is All You Need". To share that in a song is what the gift of music is all about.

Living the Junior High Life

It was 1977, Star Wars was released. It would go on to become the highest-grossing film of it's time. Fleetwood Mac's "Rumours" would go on to win the Grammy for album of the year. Convicted murderer Gary Gilmore, is shot to death by a firing squad in Utah, becoming the first person to be executed in the United States since the death penalty was reinstated in 1976. Jimmy Carter would succeed Gerald Ford as the 39th President of the United States. Disco music peeks as the movie "Saturday Night Fever" becomes a sensation. Roots becomes the most phenomenally successful miniseries of all time. Elvis Presley and Groucho Marx both die in August and it was finally time for me to move on to Shepherdsville Junior High School. Obviously, it was a very eventful year.

Anyone that really knows me could tell you that I really don't care for change. So, going to a new school was kind of a challenge for me, but in time I adjusted. Shepherdsville Junior High was an old school that was once the only high school in Bullitt County until Bullitt Central was built in 1970. After that, the old school was reduced to a junior high school. At the time, the school was in need of a lot of repairs. It had been flooded a few times and over the years the old building had been used and abused. But in 1977, it was still in operation. I went there from the 8th through the 9th grade. Our neighbor Mr. Phelps was the principal of the school. It was comforting to me that Mr. Phelps was there because I always liked him.

My mom would drive Jerry, myself and our friend Denise Phelps to Roby Elementary school every morning. Then, our bus would stop there and pick us up and take us on to Shepherdsville Junior High School. We rode bus 71 and our bus driver's name was Donna. She was a fun bus driver and she was good with the kids. One morning, something horrible happened before she picked us up at Roby. While Donna was driving some kids to Bullitt Central High School to drop them off before coming to Roby to pick us up, an unspeakable tragedy occurred. While driving the bus, Donna accidentally ran over and killed a student. The student just so happened to be a former passenger on Donna's bus from the previous year. She knew him well. His name was Rusty Stilwell. The rumor was that he was horsing around and ran out in front of the bus but then lost his balance and fell. There were lots of stories about what happened that day. Because of that, it was unclear what exactly caused the terrible tragedy to occur. In the end, it was irrelevant what caused it. Although I didn't know Rusty, he lived in my neighborhood. As a young boy, he was the first person that was close to my age that died. His untimely death rocked the whole community. Rusty Stilwell was only a sophomore when he died that day and his former bus driver (Donna) would never be the same. Her life was changed forever. After a long leave of absence, Donna would return as our bus driver, but she was clearly not the same person after the accident. It was very sad.

Bullitt County was badly shaken from the tragedy, but over time it would pick up and move on. As for me, I was still trying to find my own way in a new school. I noticed that just from going from Roby Elementary to Shepherdsville Junior High would cause my small world to get a little bigger. There were more students and more interactions. Over time, I would adjust to my new school. After a while I made some new friends but, more importantly I had discovered girls. In fact, by this time I had been noticing girls for more then 2 years. The only problem was, none of the girls had been noticing me! Ha! Sadly, young people can be very superficial, which meant that the girls didn't give a skinny guy with a bad arm and a limp much of a chance. But none the less, I had plenty of friends to keep me busy and I was having fun, so life was good.

I had Mr. Custard for homeroom and science. I had Mr. Wood for math. I liked both. I had Mrs. Playforth for social studies. All of us pubescent boys thought she was a babe, which in turn made us all hot for teacher.

During the unforgettable winter of 1977-78, we had record snow fall and record breaking cold. When you hate school as much as I did, you pray for snow. During that winter, I was a happy kid! In January of 78 we had a snowstorm that dropped 15" of snow on an area with very little snow removal equipment. That was on top of a few inches of snow already on the ground. Every 3 or 4 days it would snow again. Because of the record snow fall, we didn't have school for more than a month. It was my dream come true and a nightmare for my mom. My mother hated snow. It literally put her in a bad mood, but I loved it because I didn't have to go to school. Back then after a snowfall, we would wait to see the list of school closing on the local news. They would slowly scroll a list of school closings while a song by Chuck Mangione softly played in the background. The song was called "Bellavia". That song became so synonymous with the school closing list that if I were out of the room and heard the song on TV I would come running to see if Bullitt county was on the list. As an adult, some 40 year's later, when I hear the song Bellavia, I just have warm memories of that unforgettable winter of 1978. During that cold winter, WHAS showed what they called, "Cabin Fever Movies" at 11:30 each night. Jerry and I would stay up late and watch those old Marx Brothers movies on "Cabin Fever", "A Night at the Opera", "Monkey Business" and "A Day at the Races"., just to name a few. We loved those old comedy classics!

My favorite class in school was art. I had Mrs. Thorkelson for art. I still have some pottery that I made in her class. I also loved to draw, so that was the main reason I really enjoyed art class. For some strange reason, I even kinda liked home economics class. I remember making a pillow from scrap pieces of material on a sewing machine in that class. For whatever reason I enjoyed that. Maybe because I like quilts. I remember once the teacher also attempted to teach us how to change a baby's diaper. Thankfully, we practiced on a baby doll because I ran the safety pin through the dolls leg. Needless-to-say, changing a baby's diaper can be a challenging thing to do with just one good hand. I think the teacher gave me a passing grade on that assignment for just sheer effort alone.

One of the worst things about junior high school was health & PE. My health & PE teachers were Mr. Stoner and Mr. Marx. Mr. Stoner just appeared to be a burned-out middle-aged man that had no real interest in teaching anybody anything. Mr. Marx on the other hand, was more like a young jock who was clearly full of himself. The other strange element of health & PE class was that the two of them would "attempt" to teach us kids sex education. They would turn the lights off in the classroom and then project an old outdated film on the wall that was supposed to enlighten us about sex. The dreadful film would cover human sexual anatomy, sexual activity and sexual reproduction. The kids would be snickering and laughing, and the teachers would be chastising the kids for snickering and laughing. All in all, it would turn out to be rather uncomfortable for everyone involved, students and teachers alike. It always appeared that the PE teachers hated to teach anyway. That is why they became PE teachers in the first place. They just wanted to roll the dodgeball's out so the students could play, and they could go sit down on the bleachers and do nothing. Even though I enjoyed sports, I was clearly not athletic. I really didn't like dodgeball! The reason I didn't like dodgeball is because it seemed like it just gave the athletic boys a opportunity to try and kill you with a ball by throwing it at you as hard as they could. I was a small guy and it would stand to reason that I wouldn't enjoy the star on the football team trying to take my head off with a dodgeball. Somehow, I survived it and moved on.

Adolescence is not a pretty thing. Your adolescent years can be a maze of silliness, mischief and mistakes. Hopefully, somehow along the way you learn to become a more responsible person. Some days your life is like a sitcom and other days it's more like a teenage drama. Your mostly just learning lessons the hard way and moving on. During my last year at Shepherdsville Junior High, they took the whole 9th grade class on a field trip to Bullitt Central High School so we could tour the school and see what it was going to be like to go there. I remember the school just seemed GIGANTIC to me. The thought occurred to me, "Wow, I could get lost in that school!"

It all goes so fast. After just two short years at Shepherdsville Junior High I would finally be moving on to high school. Then it would be all about chasing girls, running around with my friends, learning to drive and getting into mischief. Hey, thinking of it that way, maybe high school wouldn't be so bad after all.

Men at Work

It's a warm Friday morning in early June. I just finished mowing the yard and I noticed that a neighbor a few doors up is having a new blacktop driveway put in. There are several men over there working on it. I'm quickly reminded of my dad because he loved to watch men working while he sat on his front porch. My dad's best friend in the neighborhood was Mr. Phelps. Anytime there was work being done around our house my dad and Mr. Phelps were always there eager to watch. They did several things together. The two of them even had their driveways blacktopped on the same day. For years after that Mr. Phelps and Dad would plan to seal their blacktop driveways on the same day and then they would help each other seal them. One year, they decided to play a practical joke on another friend and neighbor on our street. His name was Tom Collins and he was a former colleague of Mr. Phelps and the principal of North Bullitt High School. After my dad and Mr. Phelps had finished sealing each other's driveways, they came up with the idea for their practical joke. They made a big sign that read, "H & P Paving company". At the bottom, in big bold numbers they wrote Mr. Collins phone number. They carefully placed their sign at the end of our driveway, close to the road so everyone could see it. Then, the two of them proudly sat on the porch and waited for their unsuspecting friend to come home from work. As Mr. Collins came driving over the hill headed home, he passed the sign. He suddenly stopped, backed up and yelled, "Hey, that's my phone number!" With that, my dad, Mr. Phelps and Mr. Collins all three busted into laugher. All these men were good friends so that is the kind of silliness that went on in my neighborhood from time to time.

Many times, Dad and Mr. Phelps would sit out on the porch and talk about the events of the day. They would cover everything from politics, sports, their families and sometimes their old military days. Mr. Phelps had been in the Air Force years ago and my dad had retired from the Army. By this point, Mr. Phelps had been a principal for years. For some reason, some of the other men in the neighborhood had begun calling Mr. Phelps "The Professor". For whatever reason, that title seemed to fit him. Dad called him that for years and Mr. Phelps called my dad, "The Mayor". The two of them would sit and gossip about anything and everything that went on in the neighborhood. My brother Jerry and I both always enjoyed sitting there listening to them tell stories. After they had visited for a while, Mr. Phelps would always say, "Well, I guess I'll get up and head back on over to the poor house." Obviously, he was referring to his own house across the street and there was nothing poor about it. In reality, Mr. Phelps was a very blessed man with a wonderful wife and kids.

Each summer, both of them would put out a garden in their back yards. After Mr. Phelps tilled up his own garden, he would always push his tiller across the street to our house and till up Dad's garden for him. Early on, Dad would grow tomatoes, radishes, onions and cucumbers. As the years went on, he just grew tomatoes and onions in his garden. He got profoundly good at growing tomatoes. Friends and relatives alike would ask for them. Dad always said it was the special horse manure that he fertilized them with, that made them so good. He always took great pride in his tomatoes

Another close friend that my dad had in the neighborhood was Bernard Hardwick. He was the handyman in our neighborhood. Dad always took his cars to Mr. Hardwick to work on if he was having trouble with them. Mr. Hardwick even put a motor in Biff's 1965 Ford Mustang. He also put wood paneling up in our kitchen, hallway and basement during the mid- 1970's. Mr. Hardwick was a good man but was odd and he could be hard to get along with. Back then, my mom didn't think much of him. Her opinion of him would change years later after Dad suffered a stroke. Mr. Hardwick was the only friend in the neighborhood that continued to come and visit Dad. My mom noticed and she grew to really appreciate him for that. A few years later after Mr. Hardwick got the news that Mom had died, he showed up at my door with tears in his eyes to express his condolences. It showed that underneath that tough shell was a very sensitive man.

The McGillicuddy's lived down the street from us. Raymond McGillicuddy was a good man that worked hard to provide for his family. As a kid, Mr. McGillicuddy seemed more like a cartoon character then a real person to me. Whenever he was outside, he had a loud voice that could be heard all throughout the neighborhood. On occasion, my dad would be sitting out on the porch talking with him and Mr. McGillicuddy might just make this nasty sound in the back of his throat then lean back and spit a big loogie on the ground. Or, he might let go a loud belch then, just keep right on talking as though the belch were just part of the conversation. Even though Mr. McGillicuddy could be loud and braggadocious, he mostly just came across kinda like a silly fictional character out of a sitcom. Obviously, there were some colorful personalities that lived in our neighborhood and Raymond McGillicuddy was without question one of them.

My dad had other friends and acquaintances in the neighborhood that he spoke with on a regular basis as well. To a varying degree, all of these men are woven into the fabric of my childhood and my childhood was made richer by knowing them.

Lessons from High School

This is the first story of a four-part series covering my high school days.
This particular story is about lessons learned in the classroom.

The year was 1979, Jimmy Carter was the President of the United States. The price of Gas was 86 cents a gallon. On June 11th, Actor John Wayne died of cancer at age 72. On September 7th, ESPN network is launched on cable television. Wild and crazy guy, Steve Martin, has become the most popular comedian in America. Finally, on Oct 17th, President Jimmy Carter produce's one of his few crowning achievements by signing legislation creating the Department of Education.

Then, in the fall of that year I would finally enter high school to begin the last leg of my education. One of my best friends lived in a house just at the end of my street on highway 44. His name was Archie. During all three years of high school, I would stop by Archie's house and he and I would walk to school together. Once we got to school, he and I would go and stand in the lobby with a small group of friends. We would just talk and watch the girls walk by, until school started. As I mentioned before, in some of my earlier stories, because of my learning disability, I just wasn't cutout for school. None the less, I felt if I put together one final push then maybe I could get through high school. Then, I could finally rid myself of school all together. Because I had struggled all the way through, I had no intention of ever going to college. Not in a million years! My high school teachers never made any effort to change my mind. To put it mildly, I was not left with a very high opinion of most of the teachers I had at Bullitt Central. It was my experience that the students that required the most attention were absolutely given the most incompetent teachers in the whole school. I actually had a remedial reading teacher and a science teacher that would call role at the beginning of class and then leave the classroom. Each of them would finally return to the classroom close to the end of the period just in time to dismiss class. Sadly, another one of my listless teachers smelled of alcohol and was clearly so burned out that she should have retired years before. These were the kind of teachers that were left to teach the most vulnerable students. Even some of the better teachers didn't want to be bothered with teaching the slower students. Mr. Flake excelled at teaching the gifted kids. I was somehow mistakenly assigned to his class. He had no clue or interest in teaching a student with a learning disability. So, Mr. Flake sat me at a desk and told me to just copy my English textbook word for word. After a few days of doing that in his class I decided to go to the office and talk to Mrs. Phelps about it. She was the assistant principal and one of my mom's best friends. Needless- to-say, Mrs. Phelps was furious about what Mr. Flake had considered a good Lesson plan for me. She quickly had me removed from Mr. Flake's class and put me into an English 1 reading class. After that, I had a feeling that she gave Mr. Flake a stern talking too.

During my sophomore year at BC, there was a senior named Jim. He appeared to be bit of a class clown that clearly had aspirations of being a rock and roll disk jockey. Jim was kind of like a poor man's Wolfman Jack of the late 1970's. During lunch time, Jim would get on the school intercom and play the popular rock songs of the day. He would play the song "Hot Blooded" by Foreigner a lot. For whatever reason, that memory comes to mind when I think of my early days in high school. Lunch at Bullitt Central would alternate between pizza, fish sticks, meat loaf and once in a while they would serve turkey covered in some slimy gravy. As an alternative, everyday they also served hamburgers and fries. To say this meal was dripping with grease would be a "gross" understatement. The hamburger and fries were served in a white paper bag. The bottom of the bag would be so greasy from the hamburger and fries that you could literally see the burger and fries through the white bag. Talk about health food, YUMMY! Ha!

My favorite classes at Bullitt Central were chorus class with Mr. Haycock and Art class with Mrs. Twigg. I always liked to draw so that's why I enjoyed art. It was the only class I had where I felt calm and I wasn't stressed. I always used music and drawing as an escape. I had Mrs.

Hasenpfeffer for Social Studies. Sadly, I learned how to cheat in Mrs. Hasenpfeffer's class to get by. I would take a test in her class but, not turn it in. I would then take it home with me and get the answers from the textbook. I would show up early to that classroom the next day and throw my test paper under her desk. Mrs. Hasenpfeffer would later find it, grade it and hand it back out with everyone else's test paper. I somehow got a passing grade that way. Looking back, I know it was dishonest, but I felt like it was the only way I could pass. If you had a learning disability back in the 70's, then all school did was make you feel dumb. I would later learn that I really wasn't dumb, but at the time I sure felt like I was. Having a disability isn't all bad. It can make you stronger. Because of my disability, I became very determined. I would have to do things differently than most people, but I would usually figure out a way to get things done. That learned trait became something I would carry with me through the many years to come. School is much more then what you learn in the classroom. It has a lot to do with what you learn out of the classroom, as well. As bad as I struggled to get though school, I knew that quitting was never an option. I was going to finish. School taught me to become even more determined. Determination and my faith in God are the two things I have leaned on to help get me through in the classroom and in life.

Rock & Roll High School

This is the second story of a four-part series covering my high school days. This story is about the naive rock & roll dreams of a teenage boy.

The year was 1979, Jimmy Carter was the President of the United States. On Feb 11th, 43 million Americans tuned in to watch the made- for-TV movie "Elvis!" on ABC. The movie starred Kurt Russell as Elvis Presley. On June 15th, The Kids Are Alright" film premieres. The picture was a documentary about one of the world's greatest rock & roll bands, The Who. On Aug 19, the song "My Sharona" by the Knack hits #1 on the billboard charts. On September 21st, Cheap Trick releases their landmark album "Dream Police". A short time later, a petite female rocker named Pat Benatar would burst on to the music scene as she releases her sultry debut album titled "In the Heat of the Night". Then, in November of that year, Pink Floyd's epic album "The Wall" is released and goes on to sell 6 million copies in just the first 2 weeks.

And even though I was just a sophomore in 1979, I had big dreams of pursuing a career in music of my own.

My memories about high school were much more centered around the extracurricular activities that were going on in my life other than school. Things like going to concerts and dreaming of becoming a rock star. My friend Randy and I went to see bands like REO Speedwagon, Triumph, Billy Squier, The Who and 38 Special among many others. We would always leave the concert all fired up and dream about having our own band. Never mind the fact that I couldn't play an instrument. Obviously, I was very naive. I was so naive, that even though I couldn't sing, I was convinced I would front a rock & roll band someday. I would be the singer of the band and Randy would be the drummer. While Randy was building his drum set to become the next Keith Moon or Neil Peart, I was buying a PA system with huge speakers so I could become the next Roger Daltrey.

We had put the PA on layaway, and I was making payments on it. Like all respectable rock stars, I began experimenting with drugs and alcohol. When it came to drugs, just taking a few pills or smoking a little marijuana was as far as I cared to go. Hey, you can get comfortably numb on just marijuana. Even Cheech and Chong proved that.

By 1980, I was a Junior in high school and academically I was still struggling to make my way. It was around this time that I heard of something called, "Junior, Senior Cut Day". It was an unofficial day that the students set aside every year to cut school for the day. Well, most days I went to school, but I can honestly say that I did cut school a few days while I was at Bullitt Central. If I decided to cut school, I had to stay away from my neighborhood because there were several educators that lived on my street. They all knew my parents and would turn me in. Once, Randy and another friend named Warren and I cut school so we could go buy a car stereo for Warren's Chevy Nova. Then, we just drove around the rest of the day with the windows down while blasting rock music on his new car stereo.

On December 9th, 1980, right after I got up to go to school, my mom shared the terrible news that John Lennon had been killed the night before by a mentally deranged assassin. I was a fan of The Beatles, so I was sad to hear the news. Lennon's death was devastating news to music fans all over the world. For days and days rock & roll stations played Beatles songs and Lennon's solo work on the radio in his memory. That is when I truly began to realize just what a tremendous thing it was to lose such an influential person to a whole generation. John Lennon was only 40 years old when he was killed. All throughout the Christmas holiday season that year they played "Imagine" and "Happy Xmas (War Is Over)". Both are classic John Lennon songs. Back then, every Christmas I would listen to the Bridge the Gap Telethon on WLRS radio. Listeners would take new toys and donations to the radio station, so that poor children in the community could have some toys for Christmas. All throughout the telethon DJ's Ron Clay and Terry Meiners would play Christmas songs and interview listeners as they came to the station to drop off their donations. I have fond memories of listening to that telethon during those cold winter days.

Later that year, Randy and I went to the theatre to see The Who movie, "The Kids Are Alright". We were totally blown away by their live performance of "Won't Get Fooled Again". The Who were the most electrifying live rock band of their time. From 1969 to 1978 they were incredible. A few months later, we went to the Vogue theatre to see a midnight showing of that movie again. The audience was cheering at the screen as if they were at a real rock concert. It was cool to be in that theatre with all those crazy Who fans. There was an explosive positive energy. It was like a celebration.

By the time I reached my senior year, I finally got the PA system paid off. I practiced and practiced, but the end result wasn't good. It became abundantly clear that I just couldn't sing a lick. Obviously, that meant I would have to abandon my dream of becoming a rock star. Sadly, I was too clueless to realize that my lack of talent would get in the way of my big dreams of becoming a rock star. The unlimited dreams of an adolescent boy can be powerful, but they can also be very misguided and naive. As a high school sophomore, I truly believed being a rock star was my destiny. But, because of a lack of talent, my aspirations of becoming a musician would prove to be nothing more than the dreams of a naive teenager. The truth be told, the rock & roll lifestyle would have never been my cup of tea anyway. My passion for music would stay strong and I would continue to be inspired by it for many years to come. I ended up selling the PA system and the speakers to Randy because he was still pursuing his dream to play drums in a rock band. For me, the pressure I put on myself to play in a rock band was too stressful. Standing on the outskirts of music and enjoying it for just the pure art form that it has brought me far more pleasure then trying to pursue it as a career.

I believe all kids should have big plans for their future, even if those plans include becoming a rock star. All plans start out as nothing more then a dream that can later become reality. Every successful person first dreamed of doing something unique, then they went out and did it. In life, we learn that not all dreams come true. It takes talent and skill to become a musician and that is something I didn't have. I am talented in other ways. I'm just not sure what those ways are. Ha! When it was time to give up on my rock & roll dream, I was totally at peace with it. I was ready to move on. I guess, I was finally growing up. Now if you were to ask my wife, she would tell you that more than 30 years after high school, I still haven't grown up. But hey, at least I'm not still dreaming of touring the world in a rock band. That's a start, right?

High School Sports Shorts!

This is the third story of a four-part series covering my high school days.

This story is about high school sports and adolescence.

The year was 1980, Jimmy Carter was the President of the United States. Feb 22, in a stunning upset, the U.S.A. Olympic hockey team defeated the Soviet Union 4-3 at Lake Placid, N.Y. The U.S.A team would go on to win the gold medal. On February 25, Bob Seger & The Silver Bullitt Band release the album "Against the Wind". The title track would prove to be a "coming of age" masterpiece. On March 23rd the Louisville Cardinals defeated the UCLA Bruins to win their first NCAA national championship as Darrell Griffith scores 23 points. On October 2nd, Larry Holmes retains his WBC World Heavyweight crown with an eleventh- round technical knockout over Muhammad Ali. The loss essentially ended Ali's boxing career.

Also, in 1980, Bullitt Central High School was busy making it's own sports history. Long before local television stations made stars out of high school football players on shows like, "Touchdown Friday Night", we still enjoyed the games, but with far less fanfare. It would start with what sounded like a hundred football cleats thundering up the long asphalt sidewalk. With the school band playing, the team would burst full force through a large paper Cougar as the players would take the field. It was time to play football. When I was in high school, my friends and I thought it was fun to go to the home football games on Friday night. I would say without any doubt that the best team that B.C. ever fielded was the Bullitt Central Cougar team of 1980. It was a veteran team with 20 upper class men. The star player wore number 12. He was the quarterback and punt returner. His name was Danny Prescott. Danny was without question one of the best athletes that Bullitt County ever produced. That year, the Cougars only lost one game during the regular season. Going to the football games and walking around with my friends, was always a blast.

After the games we would go cruising around town getting into mischief. Our team finally lost in the second round of the playoffs to Franklin County. It was the end of a wonderful ride for our whole school.

Between my junior and senior year, my friend Greg became very focused on working himself into the starting lineup on the varsity basketball team at Bullitt Central, by training hard all summer. Greg trained by putting a weight vest on and running from his house to Bullitt Central and then running the track around the football field. I would get on my bike and ride next to him while he ran to the school. Once he got there, I would time him with a stopwatch as he ran around the track. He would also run sprints up and down the school bleachers. Greg was very determined. He would sometimes run with ankle weights on as well. I'm sure Greg has knee problems to this day from the damage he sustained from running during that long summer of 1980. As it turned out, Greg ended up quitting on the second day of tryouts. He had made the team but had become very disenchanted by the way the process played out. Sometimes the decision making of a teenager can be truly unexplainable.

Much like the football games, my friends and I enjoyed going to the basketball games as well. Just walking around checking out the girls and sitting up in the bleachers watching the game and then going to Mr. Gattis for pizza and hanging out with my friends, was always fun.

The 1981 boys' basketball team was pretty good. They won the 29th District basketball Tournament. The 1981 girls' basketball team had an even better season. They were Regional Runners-up and District Champions as well.

Back when I was in school the sports teams were an important part of the student body. If your school was any good at sports, the students had a strong sense of school pride. Back before there was Facebook or texting, going to the football and basketball games may be the only time you would have contact with your classmates outside of the classroom. So, going to the games was kind of a big deal. Even the kids that cared nothing about sports would go to the games. It was like a large social gathering. Everyone would be walking around interacting with each other.

While the game was being played, there would be all these little mini dramas playing out between the students that attended. A few things you may have noticed at a high school game were things like a teenage girl storms off after she has a disagreement with her first boyfriend. A small group of girls sitting together, giggling as they point out the cute boys walking by. A harmless fist fight between overzealous students on a night when your team is playing their archrival from across town. A sugary sweet redneck couple that walk around with their hands in one another's back pocket as if they are proudly saying, "this one's mine!" Then there were the high school clicks. Like the potheads that wore the bandanas and the old green army jackets. They might be huddled together behind the bleachers smoking. Then, there was also the popular, pretty people at school that all hung together, while being careful to never let an overweight or unattractive person penetrate their shallow minded wall of beauty. Unfortunately, it can be rather sad what we think is important as teenagers. In a group of teenagers, those were just a few random things that may occur. As for me, I was rather invisible, and I would just blend into the crowd. I could be found just leaning up against the fence while hanging with my friends and watching the game.

Back then, I thought those games would last forever. Now, more than 40 years later, they are nothing more than a distant memory. Nevertheless, it's a ritual that still plays out on Friday nights every autumn at all the county schools. I live less than a mile from Bullitt Central, so I can hear the school band playing on a cool fall Friday night. Recently, I went to a game at my old high school. There were tons of teenagers there walking around. There were lots of smiles and laughter. On that night the Bullitt Central Cougars defeated their rival North Bullitt as the cheerleaders chanted, "Let's Go BC, Let's Go!" Those kids are too young to know it yet but someday they will have fond memories of how much they enjoyed the simple pleasures of a high school game together. I guess it proves, the more things change, the more they stay the same.

School's out Forever!

This is the fourth and final story of a four-part series covering my high school days. This story is about graduation and perseverance.

The year was 1981, January 20th, Ronald Reagan becomes the 40th President of the United States. March 6th, after 19 years hosting the CBS Evening News, Walter Cronkite signs off for the last time. August 1st, MTV is launched on cable television. The new video music format would go on to change pop music. It would revolutionize the way in which we would see and hear music forever.

After 12 long years of public education, I had finally reached the end and it was time to prepare for graduation. Oddly enough, they had the whole senior class show up a couple of days before graduation so everyone could practice the graduation ceremony. The class of 1981 was the largest graduating class that would ever come through Bullitt Central High School. The following year Bullitt East would have its first graduation, and that substantially lowered the number of students at Bullitt Central. There was a jovial if not celebratory atmosphere in the gymnasium as the entire senior class assembled and took their seats for graduation practice to begin. A teacher walked up to the podium and asked if she could have everyone's attention because she had an important announcement to make. As she started to speak, her voice began to crack with emotion. She said, "I have some very sad news to report." Suddenly, an eerie silence fell over the entire gymnasium. Then, through her tears the teacher continued, "Last night one of your classmates was tragically killed in a car accident. His name was John Smith." All at once there was a collective gasp that went through the entire student body. Several students began crying. The teacher finished by saying the graduation practice would be canceled that day and we were asked to leave and come back the next day. In a matter of moments, it seemed as though over half of the people in the gym were sobbing. It was almost as if it were contagious. Being in a room with that many people crying and consoling each other was very emotional. I never knew John Smith, but by the response of his fellow students, he was clearly very well thought of by a great deal of people in our graduating class. Sadly, whenever I think of my graduation, I think of that single moment in time when, we all got the devastating news of a young man that lost his life far too soon. Rest in Peace, John.

On graduation night it was only fitting that I would walk down that long aisle with my friend Archie, right by my side. We had known each other since elementary school and for the last three years of high school we walked to school together. With well over three hundred plus graduates walking the line that night, the fact that we would walk up, side-by-side to get our diplomas together was purely a God thing. For me, that is a very cool memory.

As I was inching my way through that large crowd in the lobby following the graduation ceremony, I came across my old friend from elementary school, Chet Steelman. He was a little slow and for that reason, Chet was held back years ago in elementary school. Because of that, I think he was around 20 years old when he finally graduated high school that night. He and I had been through some tough times at school together. I walked over and shook Chet's hand and he said, "Jimi, this doesn't mean much to most of these people, because they are moving on to college." Then, with tears welling up in his eyes he finished, "But, this is the end of the line for me. No one else in my family has ever finished high school so this is a big deal for me." I knew exactly what he meant. Finishing school was tough for people like Chet and I, but we never gave up. I said, "Congratulations Chet!" In elementary school, all Chet ever dreamed about was becoming a truck driver. Many, many years later, I would learn that Chet was indeed driving one of those gigantic trucks at a rock quarry for a living. I wasn't at all surprised to hear that Chet made his dream come true. I have not seen him since the night we graduated. He was a wonderful friend. I have no doubt that he became a simple, hardworking man.

Years later, as I look back, I choose to focus more on the warm memories of those days instead of the struggle. As I've gotten older, I've taken up writing stories about my life. Oddly enough, I now get a lot satisfaction out of writing stories. It's very relaxing and therapeutic to me. Just based on the fact that I could hardly spell or read when I got out of school, it's quite amazing I can write stories about it now. I guess it just goes to prove that not all of us are cut out for school. Those of us who are not cut out for it, just find our own way. In my 12 years in the public-school system, I would learn far more then reading, writing and arithmetic. Without any doubt, the most important thing that school taught me was perseverance. The Webster dictionary defines the word "Perseverance" as a steadfastness in doing something regardless of difficulty or opposition, despite obstacles, discouragement or failure."

All throughout my public education experience, there were countless obstacles, a sufficient amount of difficulties and plenty of discouragement and failures. But through it all, I learned to just keep trying until I figured out how to make my own way. School taught me that I could succeed if I didn't give up. I learned perseverance that would later prepare me for the ups and downs of life.

From cerebral palsy and a learning disability to an eye disease and chronic back pain, it has been perseverance and my faith in God that has sustained me. I first discovered those attributes in school. I would continue to carry them with me through the many years that lay ahead.

Finding God

On a hot Saturday evening during the summer of 1984 my mom made an announcement. She said, "I'm going to church in the morning. If anyone else wants to go with me then get up and get ready and if you would rather not then that's ok, but I'm going!" I had not gone to church since I was a kid. So, at first, I didn't know what to think of her offer, but, the next morning I decided to get up and go with her. My dad stayed home but, Mom and I got up and went to Clermont Baptist church that morning. That day I heard the Reverend Brother Ray Armstrong for the first time. I enjoyed listening to his style of preaching. The next Sunday my mom and I got up to go to church again but this time my dad also got up to go with us. The church is located in the small town of Clermont Ky. The town is the home of Jim Beam Distillery. Clermont Baptist Church is tucked away in between two big whiskey warehouses. When we first began attending there, the church didn't even have indoor restrooms. Bro. Ray was encouraging fundraising efforts to raise money to have restrooms built onto the church. Over the next few months, we had several chili suppers to raise money for our restroom fund. During that time, I began to make friends with some of the other church goers. Those are warm memories of a special time.

Bro. Ray had a calm, laid back preaching style that was very welcoming. Ray always preached about the love of God. That really moved me. It didn't take long, and the Holy Spirit began working on me. On November 18th (that is also my birthday) I felt led to join the church. After the service, Ray asked if we could make an appointment to meet so we could talk. Ray came over to my house later that week and we sat in the living room and talked. While sitting on the couch, we prayed together, and I accepted Jesus Christ into my heart. The very next Sunday, November 25, 1984 I was baptized by Bro. Ray at Bullitt Lick Baptist Church because that church had a baptistery and ours didn't. I remember for months after that; I felt a peace in my life that I had never felt before. Feeling the presence of God is an awesome thing. Later, I became Sunday School Director and held that position for 9 years. It was a beautiful period in my life. Bro. Ray and I would visit the shut-in's or hospitals every Thursday evening. Bro. Ray Armstrong is the best man I have ever met. He is a man of great character and high morals. To me, he is the epitome of what it is to be a Christian. He and his wife are both people that truly live their faith. They are both very honest and very giving people. Bro. Ray's wife Louise helped me to get my first job and she encouraged me to sign up for disability. Louise was always very encouraging and supportive. Ray and Louise are the most caring and understanding Christians I have ever known. They both exude the love of God.

At the time, there was a very small group of young people that were attending the church and I slowly got closer to them. My Uncle Carl, Aunt Dorothy and my cousins Loretta, Marion and Roxanne all went to church there, along with my Aunt Rose. Loretta, Marion and I were all close in age, so we hung out a lot together. The Breshear family also went to the church and I became good friends with Eva, Scott and their mom Wanda. I made other Christian friends outside the church. My friend Archie and I would go and visit his Great Grandmother. Her name was Marlene Stillwater and she was a very spiritual, God loving elderly lady. I began to go visit Marlene on my own. I always enjoyed my long talks with her. Marlene would tell lots of stories of growing up and she was a wealth of biblical knowledge. She was also funny. One lazy afternoon, Bro. Ray and I were visiting Marlene when all at once Ray yawned really big. Marlene shouted, "MY GOODNESS RAY, DON'T SWALLOW ME!" Ray was startled and Marlene just busted into boisterous laughter. She was also the kind of person that if she believed in you then she stood by you. Shortly after I became a Christian, I drew a picture of Jesus from a picture of Him in the bible and I gave it to Marlene. She loved it so much that she took it to her church and hung it in her Sunday school classroom. The preacher of her church told her that it wasn't a picture of Jesus and she needed to take it down. Marlene said, "I know it's not a real picture of Jesus. It's a drawing representing Jesus." Again, the preacher told her to "Take it down!" Marlene then said, "If that picture goes, then I go!" She then took the drawing down and walked out with it and she didn't go back to that church. She stood her ground. I felt bad about it because I never meant for the drawing to cause so much fuss. Marlene told me not to worry about it. Marlene took her relationship with Christ very serious. She kept a large print Bible on her kitchen table, and she read it every day. Marlene was very sharp mentally and I was amazed at all the scripture she could quote from memory. I would take a Bible trivia game to her house and we would play it together. I would also take gospel albums to her house and we would sit and listen to them. Marlene had an enormous amount of faith. Much of the time she didn't lock her doors. I once said, "Aren't you afraid someone could break in on you?" She said, "I pray every night that God will send His holy angels to come and hover over me and keep me safe, so I'm not worried about it." When I would leave her house to start my walk home, I would be halfway across her yard and she would always shout, "Don't spend any wooden nickels!" Then I would shout back, "Don't kill any dead snakes!" Then I would hear her laugh. Sadly, Marlene was so into God that most of her own family didn't even come around her because they got tired of her witnessing to them all the time. I was into God and plus, I thought she was funny, so I loved to visit Marlene. Anytime Marlene noticed that Billy Graham was having a revival on TV, she would call everyone she could think of to tell them to watch it. Once, she called my house and my Mom answered and Marlene just shouted, "BILLY GRAHAM IS ON!" And then she hung up so she could call the next friend to alert them of her important news. Marlene has been gone for many, many years now but I still think of her often. She was a dear soul. Bro. Ray and Marlene both played a big role in my early spiritual growth.

In my early Christian walk, I listened to the Bible on cassette for hours a day. While listening, I would sit with my King James Bible and highlight all my favorite verses. During that time, it was as if I couldn't get enough of it. It was all new and exciting.

A year or so after I became a Christian, my dad became a Christian as well. Bro. Ray once told me that my dad told him that one reason that he became a Christian was because he "wanted the kind of peace that Jimi has." At the time, I had no idea that I was influencing my dad in anyway. I didn't even know the peace I felt at the time was so noticeable to others around me. My dad later became a deacon in the church. God really does work in mysterious ways.

It's now more than 30 years later and my relationship with God is still very important to me. My wife, Sherri was raised Catholic and I was raised Baptist, so we compromised and attend the Shepherdsville Christian Church together. God has blessed us, and we bless others by doing things like Big Brothers, Big Sisters and by helping people when we can. I do wish I did a better job of sharing the positivity of God. I never feel as though I can live up to the love of God. His love is deeper than anything we could ever imagine. For me, God is personification of love. Bro. Ray once said, "Even if there were no heaven and no hell, living the Christian life is by far the best way to live." I couldn't agree more.

A Hippy's Nightmare!

One more for the road... I want to share a funny story about my friend Archie and his Great Grandmother, Marlene. Once my buddy Archie took his Great Grandmother to the hospital to visit a sick relative. The person they were going to see was on the 5th floor so Archie and Marlene got on the elevator and started up. The elevator stopped at the 2nd floor and a young man with really long hair stepped into the elevator and the doors closed and the elevator started up. Never to be left without words, Marlene looked the longhaired stranger up and down and she said to her great grandson, "Archibald, is that a man or a woman?!" Of course, Archie was shocked that his Granny would ask such a blunt question right in front of this total stranger. The man was clearly annoyed and pushed the 4th floor button so he could get off the elevator as quickly as possible. Totally embarrassed and wanting to defuse the situation, Archie said, "Granny, he is a man!" Then, without hesitation Marlene said, "Well, you can't tell these days unless you jerk their drawers down to see!" By this time, the elevator door was opening up and the long-haired man could finally escape from this Bible carrying, quick tongued, insult artist. By the end of the day, Archie vowed to never take Marlene to visit anyone at the hospital ever again. Gee, I can't imagine why.

The Sun Dial

I am a blessed man. Yes, in countless ways, I have been blessed in my life. I had an amazing childhood and I had wonderful parents. No, my parents weren't perfect by any means. They each had their flaws. One thing was very clear though, my mother and father loved each other very much. Most of the time, they got along extremely well, but if they had a disagreement that led to an argument, then it could get rather nasty pretty fast. You see, my dad was very blunt and strict. I'm sure that's what made him a good sergeant in the Army. He was very military minded. Even while at home, it was common for him to bark orders at us kids a lot. If he told you to do something, then he expected you to do it, and fast. Mom on the other hand, was much quieter and more unassuming by nature. She was by no means a pushover. For the most part, Mom was laid back and slow to anger. If you were unfortunate enough to make her mad then lookout, because she had a wicked temper and she could verbally cut you to ribbons in a matter of seconds. My dad was the disciplinarian in our family, so he probably thought he was the boss in our house, but the truth be told, that wasn't the case at all. In a somewhat humorous fashion, this story will attempt to illustrate that fact.

The story centers around a sun dial. But not just any old sun dial. It's about an antique sun dial that had belonged to my mom's Aunt Bessie. You see, Aunt Bessie was Mom's favorite Aunt. After Aunt Bessie died, Jerry bought the old sun dial at Aunt Bessie's estate sale and then he gave it to Mom. Well, Mom just cherished the sun dial. Partly because it belonged to Aunt Bessie and partly because Jerry retrieved it for her.

Well, one afternoon my dad came and informed me that he and I were going to clean out the gutters on the house. For some unknown reason, it was obvious that he was not in a good mood that day. This sort of thing was never a joyful experience and I knew that I should just keep my mouth shut and go and help him. When I went outside, he was getting his gloves, a bucket and the ladder to get this dreaded task over with. My job was to hold the ladder for him, because he was deathly afraid of heights. Dad leaned the ladder up against house and prepared to climb up. Just before he started, Mom came outside and noticed that the ladder was dangerously close to her priceless sun dial. She then warned Dad to be careful and not break it. For whatever reason, Dad was in no mood to hear Mom's advice on the matter, so he yelled, "Oh hell, go back in the house, I'm not going to hurt your damned old sun dial!" With that, Mom grumbled back something that was inaudible and swiftly turned and stormed back in the house.

I sarcastically thought to myself, "boy oh boy, this is going to be a fun afternoon." Whoever said, "father knows best", didn't have a father with a bad temper. Seeing the two of them fighting wasn't unheard of around our house, but it certainly didn't happen on a regular basis either, so when it did happen, it was rather unsettling. Nonetheless, now that Dad had accomplished the unnecessary task of pissing Mom off, it was time to get on with the job at hand. The ladder wasn't quite where he wanted it, so he moved it over just a little more. Before starting up the perfectly positioned ladder, Dad turned to grab the bucket. Unbeknownst to him, right as he turned away, the ladder suddenly began to slide. Before he could even react, "CRASH", the ladder had fallen and smashed Mom's priceless sun dial to smithereens. He stood there totally stunned and completely speechless. The silence was deafening. My guess is that Dad could see his life flashing before his eyes, I know I could! All at once, we hear the sound of the back door open. Mom walks out into the back yard. She suddenly notices the broken pieces of her precious sun dial laying on the ground. Without saying a single word, Mom just turns and quietly walks right back into the house. Maybe she planned to subject him to the worst dose of silent treatment known to mankind. I guess you could say he deserved it. Thankfully for me, it was time for me to go to work. With tension at a fever pitch, I was just glad to be getting out of there.

Hours later, I returned from work and pulled my car into the garage. I got out of my car and started walking toward the house. As I walked along,

I heard a voice from off in the darkness say, "Psssst, Jimi! Hey Jimi, come here." Then, I noticed my dad was standing over on the patio in the back yard. I walked over there and, on the patio, next to him was the smashed- up pieces of that sun dial. Coming off very humble and almost childlike, Dad spoke to me in a whisper and said, "Do you think there is anyway you can fix this?" I answered back, "I might be able to, but I'm not sure." It was very obvious that he felt terrible about his actions earlier in the day. As it turned out, I was able to repair the badly damaged sun dial. In a day or two, things were back to normal in the Huckaby household. Dad never asked me to clean gutters again.

Dad (A Personal Journey of Loss and Acceptance)

Is there a reason for everything? I'm not sure I know the answer to that question. All I know is that, nothing is for certain and sometimes life can get pretty darn tough. The first time I ever really learned that was when my dad became ill with cancer.

I'll start at the beginning. It was the mid 1990's and my dad had not been feeling well. He had been having stomach problems. He finally went and had a colonoscopy done. When Dr. Manicotti's office got the results back, they immediately sent him to see his urologist, Dr. Diperna. Just before I left for work, my parents came home from seeing Dr. Diperna. When they walked through the door, my Mom looked to be in shock. She said, "You're Daddy has kidney cancer. They need to operate as soon as possible." You're never prepared to hear someone you love has cancer. I was stunned! Right after hearing that awful news, I had to rush off to work. I went to work that day because I was scheduled to go in just like any other random weekday, but my brain was numb from hearing that terrible news and I was hardly even able to function. Because my brain was in a fog and I couldn't concentrate. As the days went by, I was able to grasp the fullness of the situation and begin to deal with it.

Dad had the diseased kidney removed and they said the cancer was removed with it. So, life went on.

Later that year, Dad had a stroke during a heart catheterization. Right after the stroke, Dad didn't even recognize me. In a very flippant uncaring way the doctor said, "He will be fine, he's just had a little stroke." I said, "Doctor, it might be a little stroke to you, but that's my dad and he doesn't even know who I am." Among many things my dad had to relearn who I was. Sadly, it wasn't a "little stroke". He was never the same after that. It was very stressful for my mom and I after we got Dad home. He was into something all the time. Once, he got the car keys and snuck out of the house to leave in the car. Thankfully he ran off the side of the driveway and it scared him, and he stopped. He would get up at all hours of the night and prowl around the house doing strange things like taking all the pictures off of the walls. He would also threaten violence. Once, he even drew his fist back to hit Mom and I put my arms around him to restrain him. In his right mind, my dad would have never done that. He was just no longer himself. Dealing with my dad, in that mental state was so stressful, I thought I was going to come unglued. It got so bad that we seriously contemplated putting him into a nursing home. We were told if we did that, we would lose the house to help pay for his expenses. We made the decision to tough it out and take care of him, until the end. I talked to Biff on the phone from Texas and he said he was moving back to Kentucky so he could help. Biff knew how stressed out Mom and I had been just taking care of Dad. Finally, over time, Dad's behavior gradually began to improve.

A few months later the cancer returned. During this time, our family got closer. Biff had moved back to Kentucky with his family. Patricia was coming up from Tennessee a lot and Jerry and Diana were coming over a lot as well. Jerry had put up some handrails to help with safety issues. Everyone was pitching in to help out with Dad. Sadly, he was growing weaker and sicker by the day. Dad ended up back in the hospital.

On October 12th, 1997, while watching TV in my dad's hospital room, I saw on the news that John Denver had been killed in a plane crash. I grew up listening to John Denver's music. He was one of my all-time favorite artists. That afternoon after leaving the hospital, I stopped by Jefferson Mall and bought John Denver's box set. Most of John Denver's music is about love and nature. For the next few weeks I listened to that box set daily. It seemed to help me deal with my dad's illness. I even listened to it driving back and forth to the hospital.

On October 21st, 1997 I had taken my mom to the hospital to visit Dad. By this point, he was very ill from cancer and was so bloated that he no longer looked like himself. After I visited with him for a while, I told Mom that I was going to go back home and cut the yard and I would be back later to pick her up. When I got home, I changed clothes and went out to start cutting the yard. While I was cutting the back yard, our neighbor Mr. Phelps came over from across the street and told me that Mom had just called their house to tell me that my dad had taken a turn for the worse and that I needed to go to the hospital as soon as possible. He then said he would take care of the mower and that I should "just go now!" I ran in the house, cleaned the grass off and came back out and jump in the car and headed for the hospital. To say I was speeding on the way would be an understatement. I didn't want him to die before I got there, and I didn't want him to die while Mom was there alone. By the time I got to the hospital, Dad was still living, and Biff was there with Mom. Shortly thereafter Jerry showed up as well. My dad was very restless and moving all over the bed. He appeared to be uncomfortable and at times he would labor to breath. Gradually as the day wore on, more family came trickling in. Diana, Chantel, Sondra, Uncle Carl and Aunt Dorothy and Aunt Rose. Hal was heading back from Florida after he got the word of Dad's worsening condition. He drove the 13-hour trip straight through just to get there to be with Aunt Rose.

The part of our family that was obviously missing was my sister Patricia and her family but, they were on their way from their home in Franklin Tennessee. With Dad's condition growing more critical, we were concerned that she wouldn't get there in time. By this time, my dad was no longer saying anything. I'm not sure if it was by choice, or if he was just unable to communicate. One thing was clear, he appeared to be growing more and more uncomfortable because he was very restless as he continued to move all over the bed as if he just couldn't get comfortable. The whole time, Mom sat next to his bed while holding his hand. She reassured him that everything was going to be ok. My dad never relaxed until Patricia got there with her family. As soon as he heard her voice he finally calmed down. I was so relieved that he lived until Patricia got there. He calmed down for a while. My guess is that he could sense that we were all finally their and he relaxed. Shortly after that, his breathing began to get a little labored. It was then while holding his hand that I heard my mom softly say, "It's ok Bill, just let go." Gradually, his breathing became more and more shallow. Then, he just quietly faded away. Patricia checked his pulse and softly said, "He's gone." I remember leaning over and kissing him on the forehead and telling him I loved him.

My Dad died at 9:30p.m. on October 21st, 1997. Oddly enough, it was also my Brother Jerry's birthday. Sadly, for obvious reasons, his birthday has never felt the same to me. After heart disease, a stroke and cancer, my Dad's long struggle was finally over. His illness caused him to struggle a great deal leading up to his final days but at the end he left this world very peacefully.

After we all said our final goodbyes to Dad, it was time for us to leave the hospital. My Mom softly cried as we walked in silence through the parking garage towards the car. I unlocked and opened the door for Mom to get in. After I got in and started to drive, Mom said something that I have never forgotten. As she wiped the tears away, she said, "What in the world do people lean on in times like this if they don't have God." I said, "I have no idea." As I was pulling out of the hospital the thought occurred to me, "never again will I have to come back to this hospital and watch my dad suffer".

For me personally, his passing was a relief. When you watch a loved one suffer long enough it can be a blessing when they finally die. That is something you have to live through to fully understand.

Oddly enough, my best friend Greg was dealing with the same thing I was dealing with at the time. His dad was battling cancer and his girlfriend's dad was also fighting cancer at the time as well. A very stressful and personal thing to go through together. That year in solidarity, we ended up attending each one of our dad's funerals. A difficult year to say the least.

My dad has been gone now for more than 20 years. I still think of him often. My Dad was a good man. Among other things, Dad taught me to be strong, self-reliant and independent. He taught me the value of hard work. He taught me by example how to treat a lady.

The last thing my dad taught me was that if you choose to take care of a loved one, God will provide a way. That doesn't mean that He will make it easy, it just means He will provide a way. Up to that point in my life, helping my mom to take care of my dad was the hardest thing I had ever been through. Little did I know at the time that just a few short years later my mom would get sick and I would take care of her. The experience of taking care of my dad would pale in comparison to taking care of my mom. I believe that taking care of my dad was to help me to be strong enough to take care of my mom years later.

So, to answer my original question, "Is there a reason for everything?" I'm not sure but, I like to think that something good can come out of just about anything, but that sure doesn't mean it will be easy. Even in his sickness and death, my dad taught me a pretty amazing thing and he didn't even know it.

Dad Made Me Laugh

My dad was old school. He was a strict disciplinarian, to say the least. As hard and disciplined as my Dad was, he also had a certain wit about him. At times, he could be very funny. More often than not, dad could be funny even when he wasn't trying to be. This story just covers a couple of those occasions.

My dad was very meticulous about the care and upkeep of his property. Whether it be the car, the house or the lawn, he set a high standard for how he expected things to look. That meant that during the summer, the lawn was always freshly manicured and during the winter the snow was always shoveled off of our driveway. He would insist that I mow the lawn so often that many times I was unable to tell what part of the yard I had even cut. Much of the time, I cut it 3 times a week. During the winter, Dad would insist that we get outside and shovel our driveway while it was still snowing. I, being your typical lazy teenager always wanted to wait until the snow had stopped, so that way I would only have to shovel it once per snowfall, but Dad would have nothing to do with that idea. He wanted everything done "RIGHT NOW". In his mind, if there was work to be done, there was no time to wait. As soon as the driveway was covered with snow, he wanted it cleaned off, end of discussion. So, one snowy morning in January, he and I were out shoveling the driveway. I was at the end closest to the house and Dad was at the end closest to the street. Obviously, the snow was still falling. Well, shoveling snow can be rather loud and since there were two of us shoveling, it was twice as loud. Back then, our neighbor had a spoiled brat of a daughter. You could say that she was nothing more than a bossy teenage tyrant. At the time, I happened to be shoveling somewhat close to her bedroom window. All at once, I hear the sound of a window sliding up. As I turn to look, the little tyrant stuck her head of the window and in a very angry tone yells, "HEY, IS THAT NECESSARY??!!" Well, to a teenage boy like myself, the answer to that question would have been "no", but I thought my dad might have a different opinion, so I thought I would let him weigh in on her ill-advised question. So, I hollered down to where my dad continued to shovel and said, "Hey Dad", he stopped and in a somewhat frustrated tone, answered back, "What?!" Then, I asked the all-important question, "She wants to know if this is necessary?" Looking at me as if I had just asked the dumbest question ever, my dad yelled back, "HELL YEAH, IT'S NECESSARY!!!!" With that, the angry tyrant slammed her window shut and I went back to shoveling. My guess is, that was the shortest conversation she had ever had with an adult. In the house I grew up in, I knew better then to try to impose my will over an adult in that way. To Dad, that was disrespectful. I don't think the teenage tyrant ever spoke to him again and under those circumstances, that was probably not a bad idea.

Okay, I saved what I consider the funniest story about my dad for last. Since my dad was an Army retiree, my parents always bought their groceries from the commissary at Fort Knox. Occasionally after I was grown, I would still go to the commissary with them. On one such occasion while in the commissary, something hilarious happened. It all started innocently enough, Dad was pushing the cart as he and my mom were walking along grocery shopping. Suddenly, Dad spoke up and said that he forgot to get a can of stew. My dad loved beef stew. As he walked away, Dad told Mom he was going to get it and that he would be right back. For whatever reason, I went along with him back to the canned food aisle. Once there, he quickly grabbed a can of Dinty Moore Beef Stew off the shelf and then headed back a couple aisles over to where Mom was waiting. As we walked along, the can suddenly slipped out of my dad's hand. It hit the floor, bounced and started rolling. The can of stew rolled for a few feet and came to rest between the legs of a lady that was standing in the dairy section holding a gallon of milk. The unsuspecting lady shopper had her back to us and was completely unaware that the can of stew was between her feet on the floor. Innocently enough and without hesitation, Dad just knelt down and reached between her feet to retrieve his can of stew, only the hair on his arm grazed against that woman's inner calf causing her to scream and leap forward. As she leapt, she simultaneously threw her gallon of milk. The jug of milk went sailing through the air before it finally exploded on the floor right in front of the totally startled woman. Obviously, that caused a huge mess. By then, my dad had a firm grip on his can of Dinty Moore Beef Stew, and he was running up the aisle. Not wanting to take the blame for something I didn't do, I too took off running behind him. By the time the two of us made it back to the aisle where Mom was, we were both cracking up. Mom looked at us and said, "What have you all been up too?" Dad said, "What makes you think we've been up to something?" Without any hesitation Mom answered, "Because you've got that mischievous smile on your face!" All at once a voice came over the store intercom, "Clean up on aisle 7 please." With that, Dad and I both busted into laughter again!

After returning home, Dad enjoyed a hot bowl of beef stew. It was a nice way to end the most memorable grocery shopping experience of our lives.

Simply 9-11

It was 2001. George W. Bush becomes the 43rd President of the United States. "Drops of Jupiter" By Train goes down as one of the biggest songs of the year. Nascar legend Dale Earnhardt is killed on the last lap of the Daytona 500. The very first IPod is released by Apple Inc. and it would change the music industry forever. George Harrison, known as the "quiet Beatle" dies in the fall of that year. In September, America would suffer the worst terrorist attack in its history, and we would all grieve as a nation. The song "Hero" by Enrique Iglesias becomes a huge hit in light of how our first responders would be tested.

We all have those certain moments in time when we remember exactly where we were the second an historical event occurred. Well, these are my memories of something that we would later all come to know as simply "9-11".

I should start with a little background of what my life was like at the time. By the summer of 2001, I had been living with my mom while helping her to adjust to a life without my dad. It would prove to be a very slow adjustment for her. My best friend Greg had become an assistant women's basketball coach at the University of Louisville. By that time, his life was very busy, and I wasn't seeing him much. Back in the mid 1990's I had become close friends with a young lady in Louisville by the name of Ann Mitchell. We were around the same age and she and I had a few things in common. We had grown up during the same era and we shared a lot of the same political views. But, without question our biggest common interest was music. Ann was a full-blown musician that could play an assortment of different musical instruments. She had a small recording studio in her basement complete with a baby grand piano, a full drum set and several guitars. She affectionately called her studio "Avalon". In the early days of CD burners, not many people had one. But, for the propose of recording live music, Ann had a CD burner in her studio. We would get together and make our own compilation CD's of different artists. With a strong influence from Joni Mitchell and The Beatles among others, Ann was writing and recording her own songs. I had never met anyone like Ann. She was very unique. Because of my obsession with music, Ann and I hit it off right away. She and I became instant friends after our first conversation. We would discover that we were both huge fans of guitar virtuoso Randy Rhoads. Ann and I would get on the phone and have these long philosophical conversations about modern music until the wee hours of the morning. We could also be found watching concert DVD's or just hanging out in her studio while she worked on a recent musical project. Ann and I were great friends. In those days, I would work through the week and hangout with Ann on the weekends. That was mostly my life during the summer of 2001.

On Tuesday morning September 11th, 2001, I was awakened by my mom knocking on my bedroom door. As I was coming out of the fog of a deep sleep, I heard Mom say, "Jimi, you should come and see. Something terrible has happened in New York City!" After getting dressed I walked from my bedroom to the den where Mom was watching the breaking news on TV. The live coverage was showing footage of the World Trade Center. They were reporting that at 8:46 a.m an airplane had hit the North Tower of the World Trade Center. There was a lot of confusion but, at the time the reporters were speculating that the plane may have struck the huge tower by some terrible accident. Mom and I too were discussing what could have gone wrong to have caused such a horrible thing to occur. Whatever had happened, it was obviously bad for those people that had been on that plane. It looked to be such a devastating crash that no one could have survived it.

At 9:03 a.m. while watching the live broadcast, a second plane suddenly crashed into the South Tower of the World Trade Center. At that very second it became abundantly clear that this was no accident! This was a planned attack. It was a shocking thing to witness. Mom and I sat there stunned! It is finally reported that both planes had taken off from Boston and that they had both been hijacked by terrorists.

Then at 9:37 a.m. it's reported that a plane crashes into the Pentagon in Washington, D.C., tragically killing all 59 on board the plane and 125 military and civilian personnel inside the building. By now, it is clear our country is under attack.

I then heard the cordless phone in my bedroom ringing. Mom and I were still watching the shocking events unfold on TV, so I didn't go answer the phone. Then suddenly, at 9:59 a.m. the South Tower of the World Trade Center collapsed. As the mammoth tower crumbled to the ground the sky was filled with a huge plume of black smoke, dust and debris. The people around the tower were running for their lives. It all just seemed like a horrible nightmare. Finally, there was a commercial break, so I went to listen to my phone message. It was my friend Ann. With a frantic tone she said, "Jimi, pick up your phone, all hell is breaking loose!" I could tell that she was just as shocked as I was from what she was watching on TV. I called Ann back. We talked for a while as we both tried to wrap our heads around all of this. Then, at 10:28 am, while Ann and I were talking on the phone, we watched the World Trade Center's North Tower collapse. Without question, New York City was in total chaos.

Later in the day, it was reported that a fourth plane had been hijacked. The hijackers had planned to crash that plane into the White House. After passengers and crew members aboard the hijacked Flight 93 contacted friends and family and learn about the attacks in New York and Washington, they mount an attempt to retake the plane. In response, the hijackers deliberately crash the plane into a field in Somerset County, Pennsylvania, killing all 40 passengers and crew on board.

Nothing like this had ever happened in this country and it was clear that everyone was stunned.

The attacks on September 11, 2001, would go down as the deadliest terrorist act in world history and the most devastating foreign attack on American soil. On that one day 3,017 people were killed, and more than

6,000 others wounded. Those immediate deaths included 246 on the four planes (not including the 19 hate filled terrorists who were also killed). 2,606 in the World Trade Center and in the surrounding area. It also included all 40 passengers and crew members on board the Flight 93 that crashed into a field in Somerset County, Pennsylvania and all 125 that were killed at the Pentagon. That Tuesday morning ripped us all from our routines and forced us deep into a state of panic, fear and utter grief. Our nation lost its innocence that day. Things were forever changed. In time, we would eventually pick ourselves up and move forward.

For a short time, in the days that followed 9-11, there was a beautiful sense of closeness and unity in the country. Gratitude toward uniformed public-safety workers, and especially toward firefighters was at an all-time high. Blood donations saw a surge in the weeks after 9-11. With an overwhelming sense of unity and a new resilience in America, there was a strong resurgence of patriotism not seen since World War II. Americans seemed to rediscover their love for their flag in the days and weeks after Sept. 11th. Many were displaying an American flag on their homes or vehicles. Stores sold out of them; newspapers printed pull-out versions. My mom even bought a magnetic American flag that she stuck on the refrigerator. All these many years later, it's still on there. I use it as a constant reminder to never forget that day. For a few short days after that evil terror attack, Americans were closer and more kind to each other. We were a more giving and caring nation.

Ann's birthday was September 19th. On that particular year, it couldn't have come at a better time. Shortly after the enormous sadness of 9-11, it gave us the opportunity to focus on something fun and positive. I knew that John Lennon was Ann's favorite Beatle. So, I had written the lyrics to his iconic song "Imagine" next to a drawing I did of her and framed it. She seemed to really like it. Again, it was a positive way to escape the dark cloud of 9-11.

In the weeks following the tragedy, several celebrities came together for a huge fundraiser to raise money for the families of the first responders who died during the attacks of 9-11. It was called The Concert For New York City. The show took place on October 20, 2001 at Madison Square Garden. The concert was a celebration of life and was meant to be a thank you to the heroic firefighters and other first responders that saved hundreds of lives on 9-11. Predictably enough, it was only fitting that my friend Ann and I would watch the concert together that night. David Bowie opened the show with the Simon & Garfunkel classic "America". The concert also included performances by Sir Paul McCartney, Elton John, James Taylor, John Mellencamp and New Yorker, Billy Joel. But without question, the most electrifying performance of the night came from rock legends The Who. They gave an emotional crowd the opportunity to forget their unspeakable pain for a while. The Who brought that crowd to their feet and kept them there throughout their entire set. For a brief moment, these surviving firefighters and their families were smiling, dancing, clapping and having the time of their lives. Music can be a very healing, powerful and positive thing.

As a nation, we mustn't ever forget all of those innocent Americans that died on September 11th. That day changed our country forever, but in time we were able to pick up and move on. Nearly 10 years later, America would avenge the 9-11 terror attacks, by finally hunting down and killing the mastermind behind those attacks, Osama bin Laden.

Oddly enough, there can be some good that can come from tragedy. For a short time after September 11th, we all hugged each other a little tighter. For a time, we were more patient with each other. We learned to cherish the most important things in life, like how much our friends and families meant to us. It is clear that we are all stronger when we are together. For me personally, it was a wonderful time to have a friend like Ann. We were very close friends and we were there for each other during the worst national tragedy of my lifetime, I leaned on God for peace and comfort, and I called on Ann for friendship and she and I both leaned on music to get us through.

Mom (Grace During the Storm)

This is my personal account of taking care of my mother. At times, being a caregiver for a dementia patient is very dark and sad. In this story I have chosen to concentrate on God's grace that allowed us to be able to take care of my mother at home until she died. The story only represents my opinion of the events that took place. It's not meant to represent anyone else's views or opinions other than my own.

One of my mom's favorite scriptures was Ecclesiastes 3:1-8. I added this scripture in honor of my mother.   Patricia Doreen Huckaby

Ecclesiastes 3:1-8 (KJV)

"3. To everything there is a season, and a time to every purpose under the heaven:
    2. A time to be born, and a time to die; a time to plant, and a time to pluck up that which is planted;
    3. A time to kill, and a time to heal; a time to break down, and a time to build up;
    4. A time to weep, and a time to laugh; a time to mourn, and a time to dance;
    5. A time to cast away stones, and a time to gather stones together; a time to embrace, and a time to refrain from embracing;
    6. A time to get, and a time to lose; a time to keep, and a time to cast away;
    7. A time to rend, and a time to sew; a time to keep silence, and a time to speak;
    8. A time to love, and a time to hate; a time of war, and a time of peace."

The following is a story about the struggle of life and the grace of God.

After my dad passed away, I spent a lot more time at home to look after my mom. She really struggled after losing Dad. After a significant period of time, she was still noticeably depressed and sad after losing him. I would take her places and do things with her. I took her to antique shops. On Sunday's I would take Mom to visit Biff and Sondra in La Grange Ky. On occasion, I would take her to the movies. She would also go down to Franklin Tennessee and spend a week or so with Patricia. She really enjoyed doing that. Jerry and Diana would also take her places and do things with her. We were all trying to keep Mom busy and cheer her up.

It was during this time that Biff announced that he, Sondra and the girls were moving back to Oklahoma. Mom was shocked and upset by the news. I understood it because Biff wanted to do what he felt was best for his family. I think Mom was so upset by it because she wanted to be close to the girls as they grew up. Obviously, she would really miss Biff as well. In time Mom adjusted to the change after Biff and the girls moved back to Oklahoma.

Once Patricia called me right after she came to visit to ask me if I had "noticed anything different about Mom lately?" I said, "No, why?" She said, "Well, I think something is going on with her, but I'm not sure what." At the time I didn't know what she was really talking about, so I just kind of dismissed and forgot about it. A few weeks later, I came home, and Mom told me that "Chantel was pregnant, and she was getting married." (Chantel is Jerry and Diana's daughter and Mom's oldest granddaughter.) While telling me that Chantel was pregnant, Mom told me some other things that didn't make any sense, so I called Jerry to ask him if Chantel really was pregnant and he said, "no". Since my mother wasn't the kind of person to lie about anything like that, I knew something must be wrong with her. Shortly after that, I started noticing Mom was having trouble dressing herself. She would go in her bedroom and shut the door and stay for an hour or so. She would then come out crying in frustration because she couldn't get her shirt on. During this time, she also over drew her checking account. That was totally unlike Mom. She had always been careful with money and balancing her checkbook. After Mom saw a neurologist, I finally took her to have a cat scan done of her brain to check for Alzheimer's. The doctor called us and said the cat scan showed no sign of dementia or Alzheimer's disease. Mom was just ecstatic with the good news. It was clear Mom was deeply worried that she had it. Little did we know at the time there was no reason to celebrate.

Once, out of the blue, Mom told me to call Jerry and ask him to come over the next day. When Jerry came over. Mom asked Jerry and I both to sit down at the kitchen table and then she said, "I want you boys to get some estimates on having central air put in this house. I don't care what it costs, I want it done!" Mom knew that my dad had looked into having central air put in years before and then he was stricken with cancer and it never got done. Looking back, I believe that my mom knew she was becoming ill and she knew she was planning to leave the house to me. She also knew that I didn't have the money to have central air put in, so she wanted to make sure it got done. It was the last big financial decision my Mom ever made. Shortly thereafter, the dementia would begin to steal her mind.

It was around this time that Mom became very sick with a UTI and she had to be hospitalized. She was only in the hospital for a few days but when Mom was ready to be released, she was too weak to walk on her own. The doctor recommended that she go into a rehab facility for a few days to improve her balance. Then the doctor told me that because of her mental state Mom should no longer be left at home alone. This left me wondering about how I could keep my job and also make sure that Mom always had someone there to look after her. Those were some very troubling and frightening days for me. Early on, it was frightening because I had never been around anything like this and I had no clue how to handle it. Plus, I was the only one living with Mom and I felt that dealing with her like this was likely to be my responsibility. I had absolutely no idea what was wrong with her, but it was obvious that she was losing her faculties. Then all at once an act of God occurred. My cousin Marion had brought my Uncle Carl to visit mom at the hospital. During that visit she told me she had taken a buyout at Publishers Printing and that she was planning to go to nursing school in E-town. When I told her, I was looking for someone to sit with Mom in the evenings while I was at work Marion said she could do it. The fact that Marion had already taken that buyout at the exact time that we needed someone to help with Mom was no coincidence. For me, THAT was an act of God.

This whole thing was bigger than I could handle, I knew I needed to call on all of my siblings for help. The first course of action was for all of us kids to get together with Mom and explain to her that some changes needed to be made. Thankfully, her mind was somewhat clear on the day we all got together. Mom wanted Jerry to write her checks and pay the bills. She wanted me to be her power of attorney.

Then Patricia suggested we take Mom to see a geriatric psychiatrist so we could get her some professional help. That was a great piece of advice. A geriatric psychiatrist specializes in dementia diseases. I believe the one we found was the best one in the state of Kentucky. His name was Dr. Benjamin T. Swanhauser. He was outstanding. He kind of looked a little bit like my brother Jerry. The funny thing is that Mom developed a crush on Dr. Swanhauser. She would get all giggly and silly anytime I brought him up. Dr. Swanhauser was a highly skilled doctor and a gifted communicator. He was very respectful of Mom. Much of the time he would discuss very sensitive issues regarding her. He could always talk with me while right in front of her in such a way that she was never offended by anything he would say. In other words, he was so crafty with his words that he could give me advice on how to handle her and much of the time she didn't even pick up on the fact that he was talking about her. Being that she had dementia, she also suffered from paranoia, so that was not an easy thing to do. After a thorough examination in our first meeting, Dr. Swanhauser diagnosed Mom with something called Lewy body dementia. I had never heard of it. Lewy body dementia, also known as dementia with Lewy bodies, is the second most common type of progressive dementia after Alzheimer's disease dementia. Protein deposits, called Lewy bodies, develop in nerve cells in the brain regions involved in thinking, memory and movement. Lewy body dementia causes a progressive decline in mental abilities. People with Lewy body dementia may experience visual hallucinations, and changes in alertness and attention. Other effects include Parkinson's disease-like symptoms such as rigid muscles, slow movement and tremors. Over time, Mom experienced all of those symptoms and then some.

Obviously, Mom was fighting a very serious disease. It would take an enormous amount of patience, love and hard work to give her the care she required. From the early stages of Mom's illness, my Aunt Rose would come over to the house and help with her 6 days a week. Not only was Aunt Rose my mom's closest sister, they were also lifelong best friends. It was heartbreaking for Aunt Rose to watch Mom struggle with the mental and physical illness that she had been stricken with, but day in and day out, Aunt Rose would still come over to help. Her support was unwavering, and she was as solid as a rock. A lot of the time, she would bring Mom homemade potato soup for lunch. Mom loved it and really appreciated it.

One of the Lewy body dementia symptoms that Mom struggled with a great deal was hallucinations. The doctor put her on some strong meds to control them, but they never went away. Some days the hallucinations would be worse than other days. Thankfully, most of the time Mom would see children or babies in her hallucinations. Dr. Swanhauser once told me that Mom was fortunate because a lot of Lewy Body Dementia patients see scary things in their hallucinations. But, most of the time Mom would smile and say, "Look at that baby over there." She really was convinced that she was seeing a baby.

My cousin Marion would come to the house to relieve me in the afternoons so I could go to work. She would sit with Mom 4 afternoons a week from 3:00 to 8:30. Much of the time, Marion and I would give Mom a shower before I rushed out the door to work. Going to work was a great distraction for me so I could get away from the enormity of the situation I was dealing with. Early on, Marion would take Mom for a walk down the street and up the sidewalk and back home. One afternoon they were walking, and Mom suddenly tripped and fell on the sidewalk. The first thing

Marion did was to check Mom over to make sure she didn't break any bones. Then Marion began to wonder how she was going to get Mom up by herself. Suddenly, a gentleman walked up and said, "Do you need some Help?" Marion said, "Yes, I would appreciate it." The kind man helped Marion to get Mom on her feet. Mom had skinned her knee from the fall. After Marion looked at it to make sure it was ok, she turned to thank the gentleman for helping her and he was gone. Marion looked in every direction and he was nowhere to be seen. I personally believe that was another God thing. Whether or not the man was an angel or not could be debated but I believe whatever he was came from God. He showed up at the right time and that's all that matters.

There were more than enough sad and stressful days while watching my mother battle her illness, but there were also the occasional humorous moments that would help us to keep going. One evening after getting home from work, Marion and I were getting Mom up to take her to the bathroom and then to bed. After we helped her to stand up, she took a couple of steps, then all at once Mom passed gas. That prompted Marion to say, "Somebody has the walking farts!" Then, Mom got tickled which caused her to fart a few more times as we headed down the hallway. As we all laughed, Mom farted all the way to the bathroom. It was just one of those lighthearted moments that helped us get through some very stressful days.

In the early stages of Mom's illness, she enjoyed sitting on the patio in the backyard. It was during this time that I started landscaping the backyard. I first hired Ernie (the maintenance man at the gym where I worked) to close in the basement entrance and partially rebuild the barn in the backyard. I bought 3 Azaleas and 3 Miss Kim Lilac bushes and planted them in the backyard. Jerry came over and tilled up the area next to the garage so I could plant things there. Then he helped me to move Mom's Amish swing over in that spot so it would get afternoon shade. This project was started from an act of love for my mom, but over time it grew into something much more therapeutic for me. Mom began referring to the back yard as "The Garden". Every few days she would want to go out and see "The Garden" to see if anything new had been added. Even after Mom's condition had landed her in a wheelchair, we continued to take her to see "The Garden" in the backyard. It appeared to bring her a lot of joy.

Every few weeks, Patricia would come and stay the weekend to help give me a break so I could go out and do stuff. One Thanksgiving Day during this time, Patricia came with her family and cooked a big thanksgiving meal, so they could share the holiday with Mom. It was a very nice gesture. Biff would drive in from Oklahoma every 3 months to visit Mom during her illness. Biff helped me to move Mom's clothesline in the backyard. In the beginning of Mom's battle with dementia, Jerry would come by the house to help with Mom every week. As her illness grew worse, Jerry came over every day and sometimes twice a day.

As Mom's illness worsened, one thing became clear. If I planned to keep getting Mom out of bed everyday then I needed to hire someone else to help me with her during the day. That way when I would get her up there would be someone on both sides of her for safety to reduce the risk of her falling. I had become friends with one of the women that came into the gym where I worked. Her name was Cathy. She told me that she had a sister that would sit with elderly people. Cathy's sisters name was Birdie Wannamaker. After interviewing Birdie, I hired her. On Birdie's first day sitting with Mom I had to go shopping. I left a bowl of chili in the refrigerator for Birdie to feed Mom for lunch. Mom loved chili, so I thought it couldn't go wrong. Birdie was trying so hard to make a good impression that she kept offering the chili to Mom before she wanted it. After the third time of Birdie offering her the chili, Mom finally raised her voice and forcefully said, "No, I don't want any damn chili and I want you to shut up asking me that!" Obviously, by this point Mom had lost her temper. When I got home, Birdie met me at the back door and told me that Mom was expecting me to bring her a fish sandwich and that she was very angry. Because of the dementia, when Mom got angry it was nearly impossible to calm her down without drugs. So, I quickly told Birdie to not tell Mom I was home. I then rushed down to Moby Dick to buy Mom a fish sandwich. When I got back home, I rushed in the house and quickly sprinkled a crushed Seroquel pill over Mom's sandwich. Most of the time, that would calm her down. She made some hateful comments to me about Birdie but thankfully after that, Mom ate the Seroquel fish sandwich and she fell asleep. More importantly then that, Birdie was unfazed be the nasty way in which Mom treated her and came back the next day to help with Mom. In a short time, Mom would grow to love Birdie.

Around this time, each one of my siblings came to me separately and brought up the idea of putting Mom in a nursing home. Patricia even came up from Tennessee so she, Jerry and I could tour the Green Meadows nursing home in Mt Washington. I did understand why they were encouraging me to put her somewhere. None of us really knew what to do in this situation. They were just giving me their own personal, heartfelt advice. I can be pretty stubborn and hardheaded. None of them knew it, but I never had any intention of putting Mom anywhere. You see in the very early stages of Mom's illness, I learned that Mom was terrified of nursing homes. During her first night in that rehab facility, Mom was convinced she was in a nursing home and she was scared to death. Right after arriving there, she said to me through tears, "Please don't leave me here. I don't want to be in a nursing home." Then, she cried, "Will I ever get out of here alive?" I said, "Mom, this is a rehab facility and they are only here to help you. Just do what they tell you. You will get out of here alive." Mom was terribly frightened of being left there. As I walked out of her room that night, she was begging me not to leave her there. Seeing Mom so afraid made a big impact on me. I made the decision that night to do everything in my power to keep Mom in her own home as long as I could hold out. I made that commitment to myself. I never shared it with anyone, not even my siblings. All-that-being-said, I never told anyone I would never put Mom in a nursing home. I had no way of knowing what the future may hold. I just knew my body and I knew my limit. I also knew I wasn't close to my limit yet and I had no intention of giving up on my mom and putting her in a nursing home, until I reached it. Thankfully, God was providing a way to keep Mom in her own home. That is where she wanted to be.

155

The physical and mental symptoms were taking their toll on Mom. It had reached a point where it was no longer worth taking her to see her doctors. I contacted a company called MD2U. It's an in-home primary care network that provides ongoing quality care for home-bound patients. They actually send a doctor or nurse practitioner to your house. They would even send a podiatrist out to cut Mom's toenails. This was a great service. As Mom's condition gradually worsened, I talked to Dr. Swanhauser about bringing in Hosparus for Mom's end of life care. Even though we were no longer taking Mom to Dr. Swanhauser's office to see him, I still called him on the phone to get advice from him regarding her illness. Toward the end of her life he was always very cooperative and supportive when I called him to discuss her care. Whenever I finally brought up Hosparus to him, he said, "I was beginning to wonder how long it would take for you to ask for help." I said, "Well, I didn't know she was ready for that kind of care yet." Without hesitation, he answered back and said, "Yeah, it's time." Mom's Hosparus nurse's name was Cheri. She was very caring and patient with Mom. Early on, Cheri would come to check on Mom once a week. As her condition grew worse, she would come by 3 days a week.

During all of this I would continue to work on landscaping the backyard. It was my way of dealing with the stress of it all. My friend Ernie brought me a huge load of creek rock. I first used them to put a border around the swing and the trees. I used the big creek rock to make steppingstone that led up to the swing. Working on the landscaping project was a huge positive outlet for me. I mostly worked on it during the weekends.

Lewy Body Dementia also causes rigid muscles and over all body stiffness. Fairly early on, in Mom's illness, it became apparent that she could no longer roll over in bed. I learned that we all naturally roll over in bed a few times every night. If a person can't roll over in bed, then in time they will have bedsores. To prevent that from happening, I would go into Mom's room a couple of times a night and roll her over. This went on for the last two years of her life. One night late in her illness, I went in to roll Mom over and it was obvious from the smell that she had had a bowel movement in bed. It was about 2:00am and I just couldn't let Mom lay in that the rest of the night. She was sound asleep. I woke her up and said, "Mom, you've had an accident and I'm going to help you to the bathroom so I can clean you up." The problem was, she had just been in a deep asleep and because of the dementia it wasn't easy to wake her up. After sitting her up on the side of the bed, I put the gait belt around her waist and stood her up. Mom took about 4 steps and all at once her legs gave out. I held on to the gait belt and lowered her to the floor. After making sure Mom was ok, I knelt down behind her and put my hands under Mom's armpits and lifted her to her feet. Mom took a couple more steps and she started to go down a second time. Again, I lowered her to the floor. I had never had this much trouble handling Mom and helping her to walk, but it was after two in the morning and she was barely even awake. By this point, we were in the hallway. I stood Mom up one more time and we headed toward the bathroom only this time we were able to make it all the way to the toilet. My plan was to sit Mom on the toilet and then clean her up. After sitting her down, I realized she was far too dirty to be able to clean that way. The only way to get all of this nasty mess off of her was to put her in the shower. Thankfully by this time, Mom was a little more alert. I carefully lifted her off of the toilet and guided her into the shower and seated her on the shower stool. I soaped her up and cleaned her the best I could. Then, I turned the water off and dried her off good. Then, I put fresh depends and pajamas on her. After that, I put the gait belt back around Mom and led her back to her bedroom. After sitting her in a chair, I stripped the soiled bedsheets off and quickly put fresh sheets on her bed. Then, I finally put Mom back in her bed. After starting a load of sheets and towels, I walked back into my bedroom and got back in my own bed. Then, I had this thought.... "There is absolutely NO WAY I did THAT without GOD." Then, I thanked God for looking after Mom and for keeping her safe during that whole experience. After telling Jerry what happened the next day, he told me to never do that by myself again. He told me, "If that ever happens again, you call me, and I'll come over and help clean her up." Well, it did happen a couple of more times after that and true to his word, Jerry showed up to help me to clean her up in the middle of the night. His support was as solid as a rock!

By this point, I had been going all day and half of the night for over 3 years. It was taking a toll on me. I finally had a heart to heart conversation with Jerry and I told him that I was running out of gas. He said to me, "Jimi, it's almost over. I'll help you a little more. We can finish this out." By that point, Jerry was already coming over nearly every day, but he started coming over even more and helping in any way he could. I greatly appreciated it.

One of my Mom's favorite recording artists was country music singer Vince Gill. Late in Mom's life when she was no longer very responsive, I decided to play a CD of Vince Gill songs that Mom had handpicked as her favorites years before she ever became sick. I'm not sure she was able to grasp who it was as she sat there expressionless and quietly listening to it. It was just my attempt to share something with Mom that she once loved.

On a Sunday night, in mid-September of 2008, I went into Mom's bedroom to turn her over in bed. As I walked into her room, it was clear something was wrong with her. She was making an odd sound and appeared to be struggling to breathe. Since it was about 3:00am, I called Mom's on call nurse at Hosparus. I explained the situation and the nurse directed me to give Mom some meds to help her to breathe easier. She could hear Mom on the phone, and she said, "I think she might be starting the death rattle". She said she would send Mom's nurse to check on her in the morning. The next day, Mom's nurse said that she could be reaching the end. Even though I was pretty certain that Jerry wouldn't really want to be present when Mom died, I felt like I should ask him just to be sure. I'm so glad I did because he told me that he wanted to be there. Like me, he had walked every step of this painful ordeal with Mom. I shouldn't have been surprised that he would want to be there at the end. I was certainly glad I asked.

The last word. The next day right after Shelly (a caregiver that helped out with Mom) left; I went into Mom's room to tell her goodnight. Without hesitation, Mom answered back by saying, "I love you." Those were the last words that Mom ever spoke to me. She lived a couple of more days, but she never said anything else to me. It was a wonderful gift to remember.

On the evening of September 24, 2008, while I was at work, I had a conversation with a coworker and friend of mine that is also a paramedic. Because of the dire situation I knew Mom was in, I decided to ask my paramedic friend a question. Her name is Bridgett. I asked Bridgett, "how can I tell when my Mom is close to the end?" She said, "Honey, pay attention and if you notice her knee's start to turn blue then she is close to death." Then, she asked, "Jimi, what is she waiting for? Has she seen everyone that is important to her in the last couple of weeks or so?" I said "Yes". Then Bridgett asked, "Have you told her you will be ok, and it's ok to go?" I said, "No, I haven't told her that." Then Bridgett said, "Well, I think that is what she is waiting for."

Later that night at work, as I reached the end of my shift my cell phone rang. It was Shelly, (Mom's evening caregiver). She informed me that Mom was having trouble breathing and I should get home as soon as possible. I told her I was on my way, then I hurried out the door. I rushed home with 2 things on my mind. Number 1. I just wanted to get there before she died and number 2. I wanted to get ahold of Jerry so he too could get there before it was too late. When I got home that night, Mom was laying in her bed and struggling to breath. I called the on call Hosparus nurse immediately. The nurse told me to get Mom's comfort pack out of the refrigerator and then she told me which drug to administer that would help Mom's breathing. After giving Mom those meds, I called Jerry and told him that she was nearing the end and he said he was on his way over. Just before Jerry got there, I remembered what Bridgett had said, I looked at Mom's knees and her feet. The color still appeared to look normal.

By the time Jerry arrived, Mom had calmed down and was resting a little easier. I was tired so Jerry went in and sat with Mom and I went in my bedroom to lay down. Mom's TV was on and fittingly enough, that night

Larry King was interviewing Bill Clinton on his show. One of Mom's favorite presidents was Bill Clinton, until the sex scandal of course.

As I laid in my bed, I could faintly hear that Larry King Live show coming from Mom's bedroom. Jerry sat at Mom's bedside with nothing more then the blue light of the TV filling the room. Every 15 minutes or so I would go in there and ask him how she was and check on her. Then, I would go lay back down. This went on for more than 3 hours. Around 12:30 or 1:00, I went in to check on Mom and Jerry said he was going to the bathroom. After Jerry left the room, I knelt next to Mom's hospital bed and touched her hand. Then I whispered, "Mom, I will be ok. Just let go. I love you." Just before Jerry walked back in the room, I lifted the sheet and noticed that Mom's feet were turning blue. I knew it wouldn't be long. Without saying anything to Jerry, I walked out of the room to go lay back down. In less than 10 minutes Jerry said, "You may want to come in here, she is nearly gone." As I stood on one side of her bed, Jerry stood on the other side and we watched Mom calmly and peacefully take her last breath. As I bent over to kiss her on the forehead, I noticed that Mom's body had finally relaxed. The disease that had made her body stiff, rigid and crippled was gone and she was finally free. Mom died at approximately 1:30am on September 25, 2008.

I had a wonderful mother. Not a day goes by that I don't think of my mom. I was deeply influenced by her. She was the person largely responsible for me becoming the man I am today.

2 Corinthians 12:9 - "My grace is sufficient for you, for my strength is
made perfect in weakness."

The definition of the word "sufficient" in that scripture means, "enough". In every aspect of Mom's illness, God's grace was always "enough". Every time I thought, "Wow, this is more then we can handle." God would always provide a way. The fingerprints of God's grace were all over Mom's illness. As bad as that illness was, God's grace proved to be greater than her disease. God didn't heal Mom's illness, but He created an avenue by which she would be taken care of and be kept safe. Every time things got too hard to handle; God's grace opened up another pathway for us to keep going. Taking care of my mother was by far, the hardest thing I have ever been through, but God did provide a way. He never told us this life would be easy. He did however promise us that His grace would be sufficient.

Take Care and Give Love

None of us really know what we are truly capable of until we are put to the test. I was forced to learn that while watching my Mother fade into the abyss of dementia. I learned how to become more independent. At the very time I was becoming more self-reliant, I also learned the importance of leaning on other people. Both of those traits are equally important. This story is about the strength of teamwork and learning to work together. Even though the person being taken care of was my mother, the story isn't really about my mother. It's about the very difficult job that caregivers choose to do on a regular basis. It's about the enormous work involved in taking care of another person that is totally unable of doing anything for themselves. The story will cover the simple and tedious details of what a team of caregivers do in a single day. But most of all, this story is about coming together as a team to achieve an objective totally in the name of love.

A typical weekday taking care of my mother consisted of the following ....After waking up, I would go and open Mom's bedroom door to
see if she was awake yet. If she was sleeping, I would go outside and work in the yard and come back and forth to check on her until she woke up. The first paid caregiver of the day would show up at 10:00am. Her name was Birdie. She and I would patiently wait for Mom to wake up. Then, we would help Mom to the bathroom and clean her up and put fresh depends and pajamas on her. Then, we would take her to the lift chair in the living room. Birdie would give Mom an Ensure to drink while I would be crushing her morning meds with a pill crusher and putting them into a bowl of yogurt. Then, Birdie would feed it to Mom for breakfast. We would then strip her bed and wash the sheets and pajamas. If Mom messed on herself during the day, which was a frequent occurrence, we would wash a second or maybe a third load of laundry. Later, the nurse might come, or Aunt Rose and Hal would show up to visit. If they didn't bring soup for Mom's lunch, then Birdie would fix her something and I would purée it so

Mom could eat it without getting choked. Then, a physical therapist would come by to work with Mom. At 3:30 there would be a shift change as the second paid caregiver would show up. Her name was Marion and she was my first cousin. At that time, Birdie would leave for the day. Then, Marion and I would give Mom a shower. If it was needed, Marion would cut Mom's hair. I would help Marion get Mom to her lift chair and then I would rush out the door at 3:50 to go to work. At 5:30 Marion would give Mom a chocolate Ensure to drink. My brother Jerry would stop by around 6:00 after he got off work to help Marion get Mom up to go to the bathroom and then they would lead Mom back to her chair. Later in the evening, Marion would feed Mom some ice cream (with her nighttime pills crushed up in it.) I would get off work at 8:00pm and rush home. Marion and I would get Mom up from her chair and take her to the bathroom and then put her to bed. Then, Marion would leave for the night. I would finally relax a little while watching TV before turning in for the night. During the night, I would go in and turn Mom over once or twice in an attempt to prevent her from getting bedsores. The next morning, we would repeat this process all over again. If it were Friday, in between caring for Mom, Birdie would deep clean the house and I would do yard work.

Taking care of a loved one with dementia is physically and emotionally grueling. At times, a person with dementia will exhibit an enormous amount of rage that must be controlled with medication. Caring for them is very stressful and over time it takes a toll on you. It's very important that you assemble a team of caregivers to help with all of the day to day responsibilities, otherwise the gravity of the situation becomes overwhelming. It's also important to have another outlet that is separate from the enormous challenge of caring for a loved one. That is why I was landscaping the yard or working on projects around the house. Doing so gave me something positive to focus on. I did that to offset the enormity of the situation. Over time, you realize if you can keep it all in perspective, receive the appropriate amount of help and lean on God, you will make it though. Believe it or not, there is a certain peace that comes from knowing that you did all you could do to take care of a loved one. I believe that peace comes from God. When it's all said and done, we are all here to take care of each other. Having empathy, care and concern for each other is what makes human beings so extraordinary.

There is an old country song by The Judd's titled, "Love Can Build A Bridge". I believe that a caregiver's job is to help their dying loved one to build a bridge from life to death. The objective is to make that bridge as comfortable and pain free as possible and to hold their hand and love them all the way through to the other side. It can be very difficult. As sad and stressful as it is, it's the most personal and loving thing you could ever do for someone. It will also change your life forever.

My Sherri (Who says you can't have it all?)

When I look back on my life, I know I'm a blessed man. Sure, there have been some bumps in the road along the way. For so many years other than having family and a few close friends, I was alone. When I found God, He gave me peace. Years and years later, after taking care of my parents until they died, I was still waiting on that elusive butterfly of true love. My many on-line dating attempts had left me unfulfilled, but I refused to give up. After my mom passed away, my friend Greg and another friend at work named Justin helped me to remodel my house. My mom had decorated the house years before she had ever gotten sick, but it wasn't my style, so I began to make changes to it. I had actually started the remodeling job shortly before my mom's passing by totally redoing the bathroom. Early on in Mom's illness she paid someone to paint the bathroom pink, complete with wallpaper covered with pink roses. Birdie was a lady we hired to help me with Mom during her illness. When she wasn't helping out with Mom, Birdie volunteered to help me strip down the vanity in the bathroom and stain it. After Mom died, my friend Greg and I removed all the wallpaper in the bathroom and painted it. One weekend, Biff came in from Oklahoma to help me to paint the bedrooms. Shortly after that, Justin and I removed 5 layers of wallpaper in the kitchen and then we resurfaced the cabinets. That was a huge job. Mostly just living on pizza and Mountain Dew, Justin and I would work on it nearly all night after getting off work. It took several weeks to get the job done. During the remodeling job, I also bought a gas fireplace to put in the living room. It was during this time that my personal life finally turned from gravel to gold. I met this wonderful lady named Sherri. After Sherri came along, my life has never been the same.

At 2:00p.m. on Saturday June 28th, 2009, I met Sherri in person for the first time at Cracker Barrel in Elizabethtown Kentucky. By that point, we had already gotten acquainted with each other from emailing on a dating website called Singlesnet. Up to that point, I had several failed attempts at online dating. As I stood there on that warm summer day, I was patiently hoping for better results. Sherri pulled into the parking lot driving a red Nissan pickup truck that was identical to mine except that hers had a topper on it. She walked up to me with this big smile on her face, I held the door open and then followed her into the restaurant. The hostess sat us next to a window. Oddly enough, we both ordered a meat loaf sandwich. While Sherri and I were engaged in light conversation, I noticed she kept giggling. I would later learn that she tends to giggle a lot when she is nervous. At the end of our meal, I asked Sherri if she would care to go to Bernheim Forest for a nice walk. She politely accepted my invitation. It was a wonderful warm and sunny day for a nice walk at the park. During our walk, Sherri talked about her son Drew and her dog, a beagle named Scooby. After meeting Sherri for the first time the things that stood out to me were... her love of animals and nature, she was very attentive and a great listener. She was clearly more interested in getting to know me than anyone else I had ever met. She was soft spoken and gentle. It was obvious that she had a very warm and caring nature. From that day forward, my life would change forever. I was 45 years old and I had finally found the lady I had looked for my whole life. After dating Sherri for a short time, a close friend asked me what I thought of her. I pondered that question for a minute and then I said, "Well, she is wonderful. I don't believe I could ever find a better woman then Sherri." After I said that, it occurred to me that Sherri was the one for me. My long search was over.

Later, after really getting to know her, I would learn that Sherri is a very strong, independent woman. Sherri is tremendously loyal and is deeply devoted to those she loves. She has profound compassion and empathy for other people. She is very gentle and giving. I know in my heart I am blessed beyond words to have her.

As a term of endearment, I affectionately began addressing her in cards and letters as "My Sherri". It's just my way of showing the respect and love that I have for her.

In the coming years, Sherri and I would share a very simple life together. We enjoy cooking out, sitting on our swing in the back yard together and going to the drive-in. We volunteer with Big Brothers, Big Sisters to help disadvantaged kids in our area. We enjoy watching fireworks on the Fourth of July. We also enjoy working out at the gym together and watching a movie on a cold winter night. Sharing sunrise service together on Easter morning. Taking a walk at Bernheim Forest, working in the yard together, going to concerts and ball games. Occasionally taking a trip together. Sitting in front of the fireplace on a cold night. Enjoying the festivities of the Christmas holiday season with each other. Attending church together. We share countless hugs each and every week. Sherri and I are so simple that we even chose to get married at home.

Sherri ended up selling her house and moving into my house. In a short time, my house became our house. With all the hustle and bustle of everyday life, we both enjoy the time we get to share together at home. After saying grace, Sherri and I sit at the kitchen table every day and have lunch together. Even though eating at the table is just a simple, routine thing, it's special to me because nowadays not many people in our country still sit at the table and have a meal together. During the summertime, we like to have my brother Jerry and his wife Denise over for a cookout and we also enjoy entertaining family at our house during the Christmas holidays.

I truly believe that Sherri is my gift from God. Other than becoming a Christian, Sherri is by far the best thing that has ever happened to me. None of us have a perfect life but, what Sherri and I have together is close enough to perfect for me.

A Christmas Love Story

This is a Christmas story of how I came to purpose to my wife. We met during the summer of 2009 and we started dating shortly thereafter. Early on, it was very apparent that we had a connection. I had never met anyone like her. Sherri is very caring and tender hearted. To say that Sherri is an animal lover would be an understatement. She is also a giver in the truest sense of the word. Sherri is deeply loyal to those she cares about. To put it simply, Sherri is the lady I had spent most of my life looking for.

By the late fall of 2012, I was deeply in love with her. It was around this time that I decided to ask Sherri to marry me. After finally making that big decision, I knew it was time to buy her an engagement ring. I then thought to myself, "how do I go about picking out a ring?" I had no knowledge of jewelry at all and I had no clue how to pick out a ring. I also knew that I couldn't afford to buy a very expensive ring. That worried me a great deal because I didn't want the ring to look or feel cheap in anyway. So, after giving it a lot of thought, I decided to ask my longtime friend Jamie if she could help me in where to go to look at rings and what kind of ring I should buy.

It was clear while talking with Jamie on the phone, that she was very excited when I told her I was going to ask Sherri to marry me. Jamie told me not to worry about the cost. She assured me that with what I could afford to spend I could still buy a beautiful ring that would convey the love I had for my Sherri. Jamie then said if I wanted to get the most for my money then I should consider getting the ring at a pawn shop. I thought to myself, "What on earth would Sherri think of me buying her engagement ring from a PAWN SHOP!?" Jamie assured me that she knew of a pawn shop that also sold brand new rings as well because she could tell I wasn't comfortable buying something used. For me, an engagement ring is far too personal of a gift to buy used. I told Jamie I would meet her at Deprez Quality Jewelry & Loan on Tuesday of the following week. It was raining very hard when we met there around 4:00 that afternoon. Jamie was so excited that I was buying my Sherri a ring and she just couldn't wait to help. Jamie had known me for long enough to know that I had spent most of my life alone. She genuinely understood how long I had waited to find a lady like Sherri. I'm sure that is why Jamie was so excited to help. I felt like I could trust Jamie to help me to pick out the perfect engagement ring and she did not disappoint. After we got to the store, one thing was obvious. There just seemed to be a thousand rings there to choose from. I picked the one that I liked the best and then went on looking but I kept going back to the first one I picked. It was this rather small simple looking ring that seemed to fit my Sherri's sweet simple spirit. Jamie said her finger was too big for that ring, but the lady that was helping us had small hands, so Jamie asked if she could model the ring for us. Like my Sherri, that lady working at the store that day was also named Sherry. Ha! Ha! Then it all just seemed like a "God thing" that a lady named Sherry was modeling rings on her finger for me to pick out for my Sherri. Also, I would later find out that Sherri's ring size is 5½ and this ring was already cut to that size. The search was over. I picked that small simple looking ring that summed up just how much I loved her.

Now, it was time to decide how to give the ring to Sherri. I wanted it to be an original idea. I also wanted to share my love with her through music so after a lot of thought I came up with two songs that I felt would best fit the mood of this joyful occasion. Sherri and I both love Christmas, so I decided to ask Sherri to marry me on Christmas Eve of 2012. Just for fun, I decided to make her work for this long-awaited gift. So, I started out by wrapping this huge box and putting it under the tree. Inside the box I put a lap desk (just to give the box weight). Also, in that box was another smaller box that she would have to unwrap. The only thing inside the smaller box was a small note that said, "Go and open your gift under your own tree, love Jimi." That year we had put Sherri's tree up in the den and we put mine up in the living room. So, then she went to the den to open the gift under her tree. Inside that box was a note. The note said, "Listen to the song and open the next gift." She and I then walked to the living room and we sat close to each other on the couch and listened to the first song I picked. The song was titled "All I Want for Christmas Is You". This particular version of the song was sung by Michael Bubl'e. We sat quietly listening to that song in front of the toasty warmth of the fireplace as the lights on the Christmas tree softly filled the room with color.

After we listened to that song, she opened another package. Inside that box I put the lyrics to a song and another note that said, "Go listen to the song and then go look under the Charlie Brown tree, Love Jimi". We went back to the living room and listened to the other song I picked just for this moment. It was also by Michael Bubl'e and the song is called "Cold December Night". The song couldn't have been more perfect for this special occasion. Plus, it exemplifies everything that Sherri and I love to do at Christmas time. The chorus goes......

"Each year I ask for many different things, but now I know what my heart wants you to bring
So, please just fall in love with me this Christmas. There's nothing else that I would need this Christmas. Won't be wrapped under the tree, I want something that lasts forever
So, kiss me on this cold December night."

That song would go on to become our Christmas song. As Sherri and I sat there listening to this beautiful song, she would later tell me that all of these thoughts began to fill her head. Thoughts like, "Is he doing what I think he is doing"? "Is he giving me a ring?" "Is he going to propose to me?"

After listening to the song, she would go and open the last box and it was under the Charlie Brown tree that sat on a table at the end of the hallway. Inside that package was one last note that read "Go and very gently look under the hut inside of the hamster cage." I wrote that one to make her think she was getting another hamster because her hamster had died. By this point, Sherri had this very confused look on her face. She would later tell me that she was thinking, "Hamster cage!" "Maybe he isn't giving me a ring"? "Maybe it's a hamster". "How did he get a hamster in here without me knowing it?" We went into the office. I lifted the top off of the hamster cage. Sherri walked over and she just barely tilts the hut up on one side to sneak a peek underneath. She sees the tiniest little bit of something black and fury, and quickly put the hut down again! She suddenly said, "Is it black hamster??!!" I said, "I don't know. Look again." Then she slowly lifted the hut all the way up. Then, Sherri realized it wasn't a little black fury hamster at all. It was a black velvet box, opened up, with her engagement ring in it. She picked the box up and just starred at it as it sparked in the light. She was speechless. After several seconds of silence, she managed to say, "It's breathtaking." Then, she started to cry. I then kissed her and gave her a great big hug.

After I took a couple of pictures, Sherri carried the box with the ring in it back to the living room and we sat down on the couch together. With the colorful lights of the Christmas tree filling the room, I took the ring out of that small velvet box. Then, I took her by the hand and knelt down on one knee in front of her. I then asked Sherri if she would be my mine forever. Without hesitation she quickly said "Yes!". Then, I slid the ring on her finger.

As you get older you realize, one of the most important things in life is making memories. I wrote this story to help me to preserve one of my most cherished memories. A few months ago, I asked Sherri, what are your memories of that night? While smiling, she got this little twinkle in her eye and said, "It was all simply beautiful." My thoughts exactly. It goes to prove that some Christmas wishes really do come true. Mine sure did!

What Christmas means to me

Many thoughts come to my mind when I think of Christmas. My wife and I both love it! It's part of our connection. Christmas is very warm and magical to both of us. It's the unforgettable memory of proposing to my long-awaited wife on Christmas Eve of 2012.

It's taking your time putting up the Christmas tree. It's picking out the old antique ornaments to put on the tree that have been on the Huckaby tree since before I was born. It's adding the perfect musical ornaments to go on the tree with them. It's watching heartwarming Christmas movies with my wonderful wife. It's making homemade candy and cookies for those we love. It's going to my Aunt Rose's house on Christmas Eve for a big meal with family. It's about eating too much. It's seeing your neighbor's driveway full of cars. It's obvious they are entertaining a house loaded with family and friends for the holidays. It's driving around at night just to look at the Christmas lights. It's the wonder of all the traditional Christmas carols. It's Bing Crosby singing "A White Christmas". It's listening to classic Perry Como Christmas songs and it's watching "A Charlie Brown Christmas".

It's setting the 3 nativity scenes up in the living room. It's a Christmas program at church. It's that Christ part in us that makes us want to do things for others to make them feel special. It's all about the unforgettable love that God had for us to send his only son to die for us so that we could all be saved. For me, Christmas is love personified. Christmas is all of this and much more. That is what Christmas means to me. May the spirit of Christmas live on forever.

My Wedding Story

This is the story of my dream come true. On the morning of May 16th, 2015, I woke up to start a very special day in my life. On this day I would marry the girl of my dreams. I had lived most of my life alone. I had all but given up on finding my special someone to marry. That is until I met my Sherri. We met on June 28th, 2009 at Cracker Barrel in Elizabethtown Ky. That was the beginning of a whole new life for me. On that day I met the woman that I would want to spend the rest of my life with.

Previously, before Sherri and I had ever met, I started landscaping the yard. In between all the stress of taking care of my mom, who had dementia, I would spend hours and hours working in the yard. It was my way of keeping myself sane. At the end of those long, hot summer days, I would sit alone in the swing in the back yard and dream of the day that I would have a wonderful lady, to call my own, to sit there with me. I sat there many nights thinking that "Someday I want to find a lady to share my swing and my yard with". Just a few short years later God brought me Sherri. Then I finally had that wonderful lady to share my swing with and more importantly to share my life with.

When discussing where to get married, to me there seemed only one place that truly fit for such an important event in our lives. That place was our back yard. So that is where we planned for our very special day to take place. I was really pleased that Sherri agreed to have the wedding in our back yard. Sherri loves our yard as much as I do. She says it looks like a park. We love to sit out there on the swing together, so we planned to get married in our back yard because it's our little piece of paradise. Sherri and I had worked on the yard for weeks leading up to our wedding. We had put down fresh mulch, raked leaves, put down more lava rock, pulled weeds and set out fresh flowers. Then after weeks and weeks of working to get it looking as good as we could, the day of our wedding, IT RAINED!

As it turned out, we had to have the wedding in our garage. Ha! God clearly has a sense of humor.

As soon as we shared with our close friend Jamie that we were finally getting married she insisted on helping with our wedding. Jamie is not just a wonderful friend of more than 20 years, she also became our wedding planner. She came over on Friday and totally set up everything for our wedding, while I did yard work and Sherri cleaned windows. Jamie even had her brother in law Jason come over and help setup tables and get the garage ready.

We chose to have a small wedding, so we only invited 20 of our very closest friends and a select few family members. My boss Justin and Jamie's daughter Gracie both agreed to take pictures for us. They both did an outstanding job.

On the morning of our wedding Sherri left to go to e-town to get her hair done. Jamie arrived shortly before 10:00 that morning to be there when the wedding cake was to be delivered. Jamie had handpicked this lady to make our cake and deliver it. By 10:30 the cake lady was late with the cake and I could tell that Jamie was growing more and more impatient about it. After she couldn't stand waiting any longer, she called her to find out where she was. The cake lady said she was in Shelbyville and then noticed that she had made a mistake and that she should have gone to Shepherdsville instead of Shelbyville with the cake. It would take her longer to get here but I assured Jamie not to stress over it, that we had plenty of time. When she finally arrived with the cake Jamie and I went outside to meet her. It was then and there that we realized that our three- tier wedding cake had fallen over in the back of her car. The cake lady seemed to be in total shock. As the top tier of the cake lay on its side in this lady's trunk, she seemed as crushed as the cake itself. She and Jamie carried the cake inside in 2 pieces as it dripped icing every step of the way. Once in the house, Jamie and I assured the cake lady that all wasn't lost and that she could fix it. The lady quickly left to go home to get her tools to try and save our dismembered wedding cake. Then I called Sherri to share this silly cake story with her. In Sherri's sweet way she just laughed and said it would all be fine. I quickly agreed and she said she would be home soon. I could tell that she was so grateful that we were getting married that she wasn't going to let a damaged cake ruin her wedding day. That is part of why I fell in love with Sherri so easily. She knows what's important and she doesn't sweat the small stuff. The cake lady showed back up with a cake bottom she made out of cardboard. She covered it in icing and our wedding forged ahead, rain, dismembered cake and all.

Pastor Dr. John Lentz is the man who agreed to marry Sherri and I. John is also a longtime friend of my sister Patricia and her husband Roger. He did a very nice job writing our vows and performing the ceremony.

Out of the 20 guests we invited to our wedding, only one of them didn't show up. It was my brother Biff and it was totally understandable why he couldn't make it. After a 4-year battle, Biff had recently lost his wife, Sondra to cancer. Plus, his youngest daughter, Kaycie was to graduate from high school the evening before our wedding.

None the less, we had a wonderful day to share with our friends and family. I was so glad my brother Jerry and his wife Denise were there to share in our day. It was especially important to me that Patricia came down for our wedding. With our parents gone it can be easy for all of us to drift apart, so it meant a great deal to me that Patricia was there. I so wish that Biff could have been there as well. Along with Patricia was her husband Roger. For fun, they brought along their little dachshund puppy. His name is Mr. Cash. He was lots of fun running around keeping everyone smiling. Like any puppy with unlimited energy and a streak of mischief, Mr. Cash ran between our legs right as we were saying our vows.

Aunt Rose and Hal were able to come and that was the next best thing to my mom being there. Also, having my childhood friend Greg and his wife there meant more to me than words could ever say. Mrs. Phelps from across the street surprised me by showing up. My boss Justin and my good friends Harley and Joan from the Y all came. These are all truly special people that have seen me through a lot in my life and I felt blessed that they all came to see Sherri and I get married. I was happy for Sherri that her sister Robin and her best friend Lisa came to share in our very special day as well. Sherri and I neither are not comfortable being the center of attention. But I must admit, it was very nice to have our friends and family make us feel so special for a day.

I waited for many years to find a lady as giving, gentle and loving as Sherri. She was most definitely worth the wait. We are both simple people and we had a beautifully simple wedding. I look forward to many happy years together. It was a truly wonderful day.

Friends are Friends Forever

I once overheard this overzealous blow hard at the gym bragging to a member that he had six hundred friends on Facebook. After finally growing tired of this shallow conversation, I piped up and abruptly said, "You don't have six hundred friends." He said, "Yes I do." I then asked him a simple question, "Are you saying that if you're car broke down on the side of the road at 2:00am, there are six hundred different friends you could call that would come and get you?". He laughed and said, "Hey, I didn't say that! I replied, "Then, you don't have six hundred friends." Sadly, in the age of Facebook, the word "friend" can be reduced to something as meaningless as an old high school acquaintance you haven't seen or talked to in more than 25 years.

A friend is something far different then that. A friend is something very special. A true friend is by your side through the good times and bad. We can never have enough friends. Have you ever asked yourself, "I wonder just how many friends I really have?" Unless you are enormously blessed, the answer to that question may make you sad. Because the truth be told, most of us have far more acquaintances then we have friends. The American poet
Maya Angelou once said, "There's a marked difference between acquaintances and friends. Most people really don't become friends. They become deep and serious acquaintances. But in a friendship, you get to know the spirit of another person; and your values coincide."

Even though I am blessed enough to have more than a handful of friends, this particular story will focus on just one of them. She is my female friend of more than 20 years and her name is Jamie. Depending on who you ask, there are differing opinions on whether men and women can be friends without the issue of sexual attraction getting in the way. I believe that my friend Jamie and I are living proof that it is indeed possible for men and women to just be friends. I first met Jamie at the Bullitt County

YMCA. The first time I ever saw her, she was a rather comical looking sight. She had stuffed herself into a red windbreaker with the hood pulled over her head and tied tight under her chin. There was nothing showing but her eyes, nose and mouth. She was obviously new to the gym and uncomfortable about it. With the intensity of an olympic athlete, Jamie was working out hard and sweating profusely. Jamie looked as though she were trying to hide and go unnoticed. Her plan would not work. She also looked as if she might overheat so I took her a cup of water. I offered her a drink and started with some light conversation. As they say, that was the beginning of a beautiful friendship. In time I would learn that Jamie was married and had one child. A beautiful little 7-year-old girl named Jordan. When Jamie first joined the Y, she was overweight and fiercely determined to get in shape. I guided her toward a more efficient workout routine that would help Jamie to reach her goal. In time, she lost a lot of weight.

Shortly thereafter, Jamie was pregnant with her son. His name is Tres. I drew a picture of her beautiful baby boy, framed it and gave it to her. She loved it. In the coming years, Jamie would move to Michigan and then to Kansas with her husband and the kids before eventually moving back to Kentucky. During their travels, she would go on to have another daughter, her name is Gracie. That little girl is amazing. She was born with this incredible giving spirit. While they lived away, Jamie and I would write from time to time to stay in touch. During that time, I would lose my dad to cancer. I would then take care of my mom for years before losing her to dementia. While Jamie and her family were living in Kansas City, I met my wife to be, Sherri. After years of being alone, my life was finally full of love and romance. I didn't find true love until later in life. I was in my mid 40's when I met Sherri. After years of struggle, everything finally felt fresh and new. At that time, my whole world was on cloud nine. In the meantime, my friend Jamie was going through some tough stuff. Shortly before moving back to Kentucky, Jamie lost her Dad to cancer. That was very hard on her, but Jamie was excited with the news that she and and her husband were moving their family back. After returning home to Kentucky, Jamie and I resumed our friendship. At the time, I told Jamie that I was planning to propose to my beautiful girlfriend, Sherri. Jamie was so excited for me.

She even helped me through the process of picking out an engagement ring for Sherri. It was a truly joyous time in my life.

Unbeknownst to me at the time, my friend Jamie's marriage of 20 plus years was falling apart around her. Jamie's husband was leaving her. To say Jamie was crushed would be an understatement. Sherri and I were deeply worried about her for a long time. While mourning the loss of her marriage, Jamie insisted on being the wedding planner for Sherri and I. We decided not to push the issue and we just let her do it. Largely because of Jamie, Sherri and I enjoyed a beautiful small wedding at our home.

Jamie is a strong Christian. She devotes much of her time to God's work. Among many other things, you could find Jamie taking food to feed the homeless or raising money to help prevent sex trafficking. Down through the years, Jamie has tirelessly devoted countless hours helping other people in a variety of ways. She currently makes her living working as a caregiver. I'm sure she does an amazing job at it because she has tremendous compassion and empathy for other people.

After years of devoting her life to God's work, Jamie finally found love again. His name is Mark Bell and he and Jamie will become husband and wife on April 21st, 2018. Sherri and I are both very happy for them. I have been teasing Jamie that after they wed, she will become Miss Jamie Bell, which obviously sounds like a southern belle from the deep south. It is my hope that my southern bell friend, has found her Rhett Butler to spend the rest of her life with. If she is as good a wife as she is a friend, then Mark will be a very happy man for the rest of his life.

Throughout our friendship, Jamie and I have seen each other through a lot of trials and tribulations. We have laughed and hugged each other through the good times and prayed and cried with each other through the bad times. For well over 20 years, we have offered each other nothing more than love, encouragement and genuine support. When life gets tough, you realize those things aren't easy to find. It has been said that a person who finds a true friend has found a priceless treasure. I guess that makes me a wealthy man!

Sherri, Jamie & Jimi

Halloween at the Movies

The film "Halloween" from 1978. The first "Alien" movie from 1979. A psychological horror film titled "When a Stranger Calls". The African doll in "Trilogy of Terror". The low budget horror movie "It's Alive!" These are all horror movies that my friends and I became enthralled with when we were teenagers.

For some strange reason, teenage boys become interested in watching horror movies. Most of these such movies are very simplistic and similar in nature. There is usually some knife wielding crazy man or a blood thirsty monster that ends up chasing down an unsuspecting woman in-an- attempt to kill her. Inevitably, the woman would always fall down while trying to escape the assailant. That would usually end with her demise. A good deal of these kindS of movies have a poor storyline and are filled with lots of gratuitous violence and nonsense.

Looking back, the only one of those movies that was a quality product was the science fiction, horror film "Alien". During my sophomore year of high school, my friend Randy and I couldn't wait to see that movie. His mom agreed to take us. Obviously, teenagers don't want to be seen with their parents so, not to cramp our style, his mom and sister agreed to sit in a different section of the theatre then us. I wasn't really a science fiction fan, but I was really looking forward to seeing this film. The movie was very dark and suspenseful, but I was enjoying it. Early in the film, the prenatal alien violently ripped out of the chest of a helpless astronaut. It became the most talked about scene in the film and it just totally freaked Randy out. He was so shaken by the scene that he turned to me and said, "Jimi, I've got to get out of here!", and then he left the theatre and went out to the lobby. After being gone for a while, Randy finally returned and quietly sat back down next to me. He leaned over and sheepishly asked, "Have I missed anything?" I said, "No". Less then a minute later, the blood thirsty alien violently ate a crew member on the spaceship. Without hesitation, Randy got up and left the theatre again. After a long period of time, he finally returned to his seat and watched the rest of the movie. When the movie was over, we met back up with his mom and sister. The two of them were so shaken by the film that they suggested that we immediately go and see another movie. So, we went right back in the theatre and watched the James Bond film, "Moonraker". That was the first and only time I've ever seen two movies in the theatre on the same day.

Now all these many years later, my wife and I enjoy watching classic horror films around Halloween every year. During the month of October, we fill each weekend with classic ghoulish films like "Psycho", "The Birds" or the first "Alien" movie. We always make room to watch the original 1931 universal picture "Frankenstein". We may even spend a weekend watching the giants of the silver screen, "King Kong" from 1933 and "Godzilla" from 1954. It's always fun to watch "The Ghost and Mr. Chicken" starring Don Knotts or the Abbott And Costello film "Hold That Ghost!". It's also a great time to enjoy Michael Jackson's Thriller. Obviously, Halloween isn't complete if we haven't watched "It's the Great Pumpkin, Charlie Brown". We may even throw in a corny episode of "Ultraman" or "The Munster's", just for good measure. It's all in good fun, of course. For me, these things have become just as routine as the leaves that change every fall. Autumn has become our time to enjoy a nostalgic Halloween from yesteryear.

A Wise Man Once Said....

"If you haven't learned the meaning of friendship, you really haven't
learned anything."
Muhammad Ali

"True friends are trustworthy. Being trustworthy is a trait that is essential for understanding that the deepest relationships are the ones in which we can confide in each other. Trustworthy friends remind you that
you are not alone and empower you to be a better person."

As I grow older, a few things have become very clear. In this ever changing, fast paced world, it is increasingly more and more difficult to find and maintain quality friendships. When I was a kid, I grew up in a neighborhood with lots of other kids. Because of that fact, I grew up with an assortment of different friends. All throughout school I also had a variety of friends as well. I think as you get older, you come to realize that it is far more challenging to find and maintain friendships. Because of that fact, you learn the enormous value of having a true friend. If you have a true friend, you have something money can't buy, because in a sea of billions of people, you've found one person who sees the positive things about you when you don't even see them yourself.

That brings me to one of my true friends. His name is Harley Wise and believe it or not, he is one of the wisest men I know. You might be asking, other than his name, what makes Harley Wise so wise? Well, he is wise because he clearly has above average intelligence and he also has a great deal of common sense. A lot of people either have book sense or common sense, but most people do not have both. Harley has the intelligence and skill to wire a house and the know how to do your taxes, but that in itself is not what makes Harley Wise so wise. He has also accumulated years and years of life experiences from the school of hard knocks. He spends a lot of his free time giving to the poor and the less fortunate. Along with his intelligence and common sense, Harley also has a very genuine, moral compass that clearly defines who he is. That moral compass comes from his upbringing and from his strong Christian faith. Those are the real things that make Harley Wise so wise.

Harley and I first met several years ago at the Bullitt County YMCA and became close friends. At the time, his dad was in the throes of Alzheimer's disease and Harley was extremely stressed dealing with it. Harley just needed someone to talk to about it and I was a willing listener. Because I had already had some experience dealing with a loved one with dementia, I could empathize with the situation he was in. He would come up to the Y to work out and for hours at a time, I would listen to him talk about his dad's illness. I think talking about it helped him to destress. In time, I would learn that Harley and I have a lot of similarities. Our dads were both very strict disciplinarians. Harley and I are close to the same age and we were both looking for a friend. I am a conservative democrat and Harley is a self-professed liberal republican. There can't be more than two of those in the whole United States and the other one is his wife. Harley and I actually share a lot of the same political views. We've been known to have some long, in depth political conversations. Harley is also a great source of advice. But, don't ask him something unless you want his honest, unadulterated opinion, because he will give the blunt truth and sometimes the truth hurts. He may follow up his blunt answer by saying, "Hey, you asked!" If you're looking for a politically correct answer, then you would clearly be asking the wrong guy.

Harley is a retired middle school principal who has become an avid exercise enthusiast. To say he does everything to the extreme would be an absolute understatement. He was once nearly 400 pounds because he ate an enormous amount of food. After joining the Y, he became very focused on losing the extra weight. He has an addictive personality. You could say he went from a food addiction to an exercise addiction. Harley was so determined that he lost nearly 200 pounds in about a year and a half. Now, he is such an avid bicyclist that he routinely participates in 100-

mile bike events throughout the spring, summer and fall. Like I said, Harley does EVERYTHING to the extreme.

Harley also has an insatiable desire to help others as his 30 plus years working in education would prove. After retiring from his middle school principal position, Harley discovered that he still had entirely too much drive left to just fish and exercise all the time, so he started working again. He got a job working for Child Protective Services. He loves it! His job is to write a detailed summary and complete the legal paperwork so that abused and neglected children are finally adopted. He refers to it as a "happy ending" because those abused children are finally adopted by parents that really want them. Harley calls it, "the best job" he ever had. He clearly gets a great deal of satisfaction from helping others.

One of the added benefits to becoming Harley's friend is that you also become friends with his wife, Joan. They are a package deal. Joan is a truly wonderful lady. Harley and Joan have 3 children and 6 grandchildren. Harley and Joan do everything together. You rarely see one without the other. She even came along with him last summer to help him put vinyl siding on the barn in my backyard. They exemplify true partnership and teamwork. After 40 years of marriage, Harley is still crazy about Joan. He tells me that on a regular basis. They are excellent role models for the longevity of marriage. At the Y a few years ago, I broke the news to Harley that Sherri and I were getting married, he quickly jumped off the Arc Trainer he was on and ran all the way across the wellness center to tell Joan the good news. He was just absolutely ecstatic with enthusiasm. I had no idea that news would have made him so happy.

Harley and his wife are also heavily involved in Community Ministries at their church. It's a program dedicated to feeding the poor and homeless. They gather up food that is donated from local businesses throughout the week and then it's distributed to the poor and homeless in our community. It is very time consuming and labor-intensive work. Jesus once taught his disciples that faith without works is dead. Harley clearly feels that you put action behind your beliefs. I believe that is exactly what Jesus taught us to do.

Harley has helped me with a few handyman jobs around my house. Instead of a "Jack of all trades", he is kind of a "Harley of all trades", but for me, Harley is far, far more than that. Harley is a tried and true friend. He has been there to help me through some dark and difficult days. When a friend is in need, you run toward them not away from them. Harley has always been a standup guy in that regard. I've always appreciated that. I've tried to lend my support to him through some pretty difficult days as well. I am truly honored to call Harley Wise my friend.

It was once said, "True friends are selfless. They are supportive, encouraging and they genuinely care about your wellbeing. A true friend is able to understand their own life experiences but are not consumed by their own problems. Instead, they take action to help solve the problems of others."

Now that my friend, is what really makes Harley Wise so wise.

The Road to Ethan

During the summer of 2013, I had what's called a Reclast infusion done to treat the osteoporosis that I had recently been diagnosed with. Well, to put it mildly, I suffered severe side effects from that drug. Everything from tremendous joint and muscle pain, night terrors and insomnia to numbness and tingling in my arms and legs. Those side effects lasted for months. Then, I injured my back doing a landscaping job. For a significant amount of time after that, I was in a great deal of pain. For a while, it was as if my whole world came to a grinding halt. Because of the back pain, I then began experiencing anxiety and depression. I ended up seeing a physical therapist for my back pain and a psychologist for my depression. It was a very tough period in my life, but I learned a lot from it. After some intense therapy and a great deal of inner reflection, I began to gradually regain my quality of life. It was during this time that I decided I wanted to do something to make a difference in the world around me. Regardless of how small, I wanted to make a positive contribution to my community. At that stage of my life, I was 50 years old and had never fathered any children. By the time that Sherri and I met, she was beyond her childbearing years. The fact that I was never fortunate enough to have children would eventually make me more determined to help a child in some way. It was my desire to at least give stability and guidance to a disadvantaged child. But would my wife agree to go along and help me to pursue my idea of helping someone in this way?

After a lot of thought, I came up with the idea of volunteering to help a disadvantaged youth through a mentoring program in my community. I decided to ask Sherri if she would be interested in doing it with me, as a couple. When I first brought it up, she looked at me as if I had lost my mind. Obviously, she knew that taking on something like that would take huge commitment. Thankfully, Sherri also knew how much it meant to me to make a difference in a child's life, since I was never blessed to have my known children. I know it wasn't an easy thing to commit to. In early discussions about it Sherri seemed rather indifferent about the whole idea. I gave her time to pounder it and eventually she came around to the idea.

To agree to mentor someone else's child is a huge responsibility. It wasn't something that either of us were going to take for granted. The first child we were matched with was a 14-year-old boy from Shepherdsville. He had a lot of anger problems and he suffered from autism Asperger. He was very challenging to deal with, but we were determined to hang in there with him. After having him for 6 months, his mother abruptly pulled him out of the program and moved away. We were just beginning to make a little bit of progress with him and when it suddenly ended, and Sherri took it hard. For a while she wanted nothing else to do with the program. I gave her a couple of months to get over being jolted that way. I still felt a desire to help a child so I asked her if she would like to try again. After a lot of careful consideration, she reluctantly agreed to take on another child in need. Sherri and I are very similar, and I knew if she chose to help another child that she would be all in and give it a hundred percent. So, I contacted the organization again to start the process of getting a new match. Then with baited enthusiasm, we patiently waited to help another little boy. In time, we would learn that the next little boy was very special. His name is Ethan. He is a very unique and special young man. I believe that being matched up with Ethan was a God thing. Ethan's birthday is May 5th. My dad was also born on May 5th. Plus, the last 4 digits of Ethan's mothers phone number are the same as my favorite Aunt's phone number. I personally do not believe those things are a mere coincidence. For me, that was God's way of letting me know that we were meant to be in Ethan's life. In some ways, Ethan appears to be wise beyond his years. Even though he struggles some at school, he is clearly an intelligent young man. When we first met Ethan, he was just 10 years old and he was already talking about going to college when he got older. I remember telling Sherri that I believe that, "Ethan has a high ceiling". In other words, he has tremendous potential to succeed in whatever he chooses to put his mind too.

The road to Ethan was well worth the work it took to get to him. Our time with Ethan would prove to be a beautiful journey of wonder and hope.

After two years of sharing activities with this impressive 12-year-old boy, a few questions come to mind.... "Is spending a fun afternoon every other week with a him enough to make a positive difference in his life?", "Can this 12-year-old boy tell how much we care about him?" Or, "Are we able to make any impact on him at all?" I was never blessed with being a parent and I know that parenting is way more involved than just being a mentor to a child, but I'm sure responsible parents everywhere ask themselves those same kinds of questions.

All I can really do is look at it from what we were trying to accomplish. From day one, I know that Sherri and I both had a goal and we set out to achieve that goal. Our goal was to make a child feel special. Just maybe, by merely spending time with Ethan and simply listening to him, we hope he might feel special. I'm not sure if we achieved it or not but that was our objective. During our time getting to know Ethan, I can really only answer for myself. As far as I am concerned, I know this one thing, Ethan has made an impact on my life. Ethan has a great deal of potential. He has always been very respectful and well-mannered around Sherri and I both. No matter where we have gone or what we have done, Ethan always has had a positive attitude about it. He cares deeply about his mother and his two little brothers. He is very sensitive and tenderhearted. Having Ethan in my life has made my life more fulfilling. He has become very special to me. It has been an honor to get to know him.

Whether it's just the simple pleasures of a one on one conversation or sitting quietly while watching Ethan fly a kite, for Sherri and I, it's all about being there to just offer a little love and support. After all, isn't that what we all need?

The End of an Era

During the summer of 2018, I was reminded once again of the beauty and the frailty of life. I would lose my favorite Aunt and her boyfriend of nearly 30 years within a month of each other. It was a tremendous loss.

I should start at the beginning. My Aunt Rose was my mom's dearest sister and her life-long best friend. They were very close. Aunt Rose was a few years older than my mom. They had a lot of the same interests and they were very similar in nature.

They were so close that after my dad retired from the Army, Aunt Rose invited my mom and dad along with us 4 kids to live with her and Uncle Dukie and their two kids until we bought a house. For about 6 weeks, there were 10 of us living in Aunt Rose's house, until my parents finally bought their own place in Shepherdsville. How we managed to do that with only one bathroom is beyond me.

Offering to do that, just spoke of Aunt Rose's giving nature. Along with being giving, Aunt Rose was also a deeply spiritual lady. She lived through more tragedy then anyone I've ever known. During her lifetime, she out- lived two husbands, both of her children, one of her granddaughters, two of her sisters and countless friends, not to mention both of her parents. Through it all, her faith never wavered. She once told me that when her oldest son Paul lost his leg in combat during the Vietnam war, she rushed to Washington to be at his bedside. She said that watching Paul in so much physical pain was so excruciating for her that the only way she could keep her sanity was to think of the amount of pain that Jesus endured on the cross. Somehow, that gave her the strength to handle it. Throughout all the tragedies in her life, I never heard her question God or cry "woe is me". Amid all the pain, she just continued to lean on God and forge ahead. My Aunt Rose was the strongest person I have ever known.

Understand this, Aunt Rose's life wasn't all heartache and pain. Much of the time, she was very positive, upbeat and happy. Most people that knew Aunt Rose would attest to the fact that she smiled often, and she had a very infectious laugh. I believe that is one reason why she had so many friends. As I grew older, my mom would plan a birthday celebration for Aunt Rose and I together because our birthdays were only a day apart. Aunt Rose loved family gatherings. Over the years, she hosted countless Thanksgiving meals, Christmas dinners, Derby parties, fish fry's and family reunions at her home. They were always happy occasions, filled with lots of southern hospitality and plenty of delicious food. Aunt Rose loved her family. She also loved children, especially babies.

Aunt Rose was married twice, to Dukie Crump and Doyle Wentworth. She lost them both unexpectedly. She would lose Dukie to a massive heart attack and Doyle to an automobile accident. For years after that she chose to focus on her family, friends and church. After she retired from Jim Beam distillery, she and Mom took several fun trips together.

After a few years of being alone, Aunt Rose found love again. That brings me to her boyfriend, Hal Case. Hal was Aunt Rose's constant companion for the last 28 years of her life. She loved to cook, and Hal loved to eat so that made them the perfect pair. They did everything together. You rarely saw one without the other. They took trips together, went out to eat together, played cards together and they walked through this life together. The two of them exhibited the true essence of what genuine, never ending love is all about. Even though they never married, Hal became like an uncle to me and my other siblings. We grew to love him just like Aunt Rose. The two of them made a wonderful couple. Throughout good times and bad times, the two of them were virtually inseparable. The love that they shared together in their later years was truly special. Aunt Rose's health began to fail her as she began to suffer from dementia. Even when Aunt Rose grew sick toward the end of her life, Hal never abandoned her. No matter how challenging it got, he took care of her until the end. Watching Hal feed Aunt Rose in the hospital was one of the most beautifully endearing things I have ever witnessed. It spoke of the character of the man. Hal was a man of great integrity.

Hal was a very calm, slow paced gentleman. He enjoyed wheeling and dealing and finding a good bargain. He loved to trade cars, knives and guns. He loved to buy a vehicle, fix it up a little and resell it for more then he gave for it. I still drive a little Nissan pickup truck that Hal sold me a few years ago.

Hal was also a prolific storyteller. With a slow southern drawl and a sharp wit, he could keep you entertained by sharing stories of his 87 years of living. He would share stories of growing up being the son of a sharecropper. He would share stories of his old military days and he might tell you a few tails of working on the railroad. Stories of hunting and camping or vacationing with his wife of more than 30 years were all things he loved to share.

Hal lived life his way. A few years ago, he was diagnosed with cancer. He chose to do nothing about it and keep living his life. He rarely spoke of it and never complained about it. As his health declined, his main focus was still to take care of Aunt Rose and make sure she was ok. The two of them just continued to enjoy their life together by playing solitaire and going out to eat at Cracker Barrel. Hal and Rose also enjoyed watching Jeopardy and the Gaither's gospel music show every Saturday night. The two of them shared a simple life that exemplified true love and companionship. Hal would finally lose Rose on July 5th, 2018. He sent flowers to the funeral home with a card that simply read, "I love you Rose, and I will see you soon." He was deeply saddened by the loss and never really recovered from it.

Hal was very determined and fiercely independent all the way to the end of his life. After Aunt Rose died Hal was left to live alone. Because of his failing health, it had become abundantly clear that it was unsafe for him to live alone. I became deeply concerned about Hal's safety. I would go visit him daily, in an attempt to get him to move in with me and my wife. After a lot of pleading and encouragement, he began to consider making a change. In his final days, Hal finally agreed to come and live with my wife and I, so we could take care of him until he died. Even though he was hurting, Hal refused to take any pain medication. He didn't like how it made him feel and he wanted his mind to be clear. As he prepared to die, he made all the important phone calls to get his affairs in order. In the meantime, we were bringing Hal whatever food he asked for and getting him anything else he wanted to help him to be as comfortable as possible. We pulled from all the resources that Hosparus had to offer to make sure he got the best possible care. At the end, I wanted Hal to feel loved and I didn't want him to die alone.

On the last night of his life, I helped him to the bathroom and then to bed. Once again, I offered to give him his pain medication and once again, he refused. At this point, Hal was extremely weak and very sick. After helping him into the bed, I walked to his door and said, "Goodnight Hal". He replied by saying, "Goodnight Jim". Then in almost a victorious tone he said, "Tomorrow! Tomorrow will be a better day!" I said, "It sure will be, Hal." The next day, Aug. 15, 2018 at 12:40am Hal Case passed away. He was right, his tomorrow was a better day indeed. Hal was ready to go. At the end, there was no struggle at all. I sat at his bedside holding his hand as he softly drifted away.

The day before he died, he gave me 40 dollars and insisted that I take it. He said he wanted to pay his own way. In the wee hours of the morning, after the undertaker had taken his body, my wife and I were at a loss of what to do next, so we went out to eat in honor of Hal. I took 20 of the 40 dollars he had given me, and we went to Waffle House. At 4:00am there are not many restaurant options to choose from, plus we use to take Hal a pecan waffle from Waffle House sometimes. He loved them. He was such a foodie that we felt like that was a great way to honor him. Hal Case was a wonderful man and he is finally at peace.

Aunt Rose and Hal were both very important to me and my entire family. Losing them both left a tremendous hole that no one else will ever fill. Just receiving the warm unconditional love and support from Aunt Rose and hearing Hal share his wonderful stories and anecdotes are the kinds of things that help to feed the soul. Those simple, seemingly incidental things in life are the very things that give depth and warmth to everyday living. In this fast paced ever changing world, those are the kind a thing's lacking in the world today. I was truly blessed to have Aunt Rose and Hal in my family. They will live in my memory forever. I loved them both dearly. May God bless them and keep them safe throughout all eternity.

Just a Little Getaway

Anyone who knows me well could tell you that I like to keep things simple. In my life of simple pleasures, it would only stand to reason that I would enjoy a simple vacation. It had been years since I had been on a vacation of any kind. In my mind, you don't take a vacation if you don't have any expendable income. But, my wife Sherri, had bought me tickets to a Minnesota Vikings football game, for our anniversary back in the spring. Minnesota would be playing the Tennessee Titans in Nashville in late August. Well, it would prove to be somewhat of a difficult summer leading up to our little trip. You see, my Aunt who suffered from dementia would require more and more care until she finally passed away in early July. At the time, her long-time boyfriend and caregiver Hal was also battling cancer himself. A month after my Aunt died, we brought Joe into our home so we could take care of him until he passed away in mid- August. A week or so after that, I broke two fingers in a freak mowing accident. To add a little more stress to a very stressful summer, I also have another Aunt and Uncle that are both in declining health. So, their situation is rather worrisome as well. To add to our already stressful summer, our sickly cat Tom was also growing weaker. At this point, to say that it would do Sherri and I some good to get away would be a huge understatement.

When my longtime friend Greg found out that we were going to Nashville to see the Vikings play, he insisted on reserving us a room at the Opryland Hotel. The Opryland Hotel is the most popular hotel in the southern part of the United States. It was a very nice gesture on his part to book us a room there. Sherri and I were very appreciative of him for doing so.

Our drive down to Nashville was made all the made enjoyable by listening to the fun summer music of Jan & Dean. On the way to Nashville, we stopped at a Rafferty's in Bowling Green to have lunch with Greg. We enjoyed some relaxing conversation with Greg and the food was delicious. As customary with Sherri and I, we got a to-go box so we could take the leftovers with us, as we can rarely eat it all.

By mid-afternoon we had reached our destination. After a great deal of confusion from the customer service staff at the hotel, we were finally given a key to the room that Greg had reserved for us. The Opryland Hotel is gigantic and it's very nice, to say the least. I haven't been many places but, it's the nicest hotel I've ever been in. We felt honored to get to stay there. After going to our room, we sat out on the balcony for a while. As Sherri and I sat there enjoying the view, we finished the rest of our leftovers from Rafferty's.

Then, it was time to go to the big game. Even though to most fans, it was just a meaningless preseason game, for me it was a big deal. You see, I have been a Minnesota Vikings fan since I was 8 years old and I had never been to an NFL game. So, it was exciting for me to get to see my favorite team play in person. To make it all-the-more perfect for me, we just so happened to be sitting in a section of mostly Minnesota fans. To be sitting around all that purple and gold was a great plus, it was fun talking with those fans as well. In a very enthusiastic tone I announced to Sherri, "Now, THESE are my people! Ha!" Right before halftime of the game, it started to rain. We decided that it would be the perfect time to go to the concession stand to get a drink and a snack. We always get a Coke and two straws when we go to the movies and we got the same thing at the game. Sherri also bought a bag of dry roasted peanuts. As the rain was pouring down, we stood in the breezeway cracking the shelled peanuts. While eating those peanuts, I was just taking in this whole experience and enjoying the moment. As crazy as it sounds, it was of little importance to me who won the game. It also meant nothing to me that it rained. It was much more important just to go and experience watching my favorite team play while being accompanied by my wife. It was all about making memories together. As it turned out, the Minnesota Vikings defeated the Tennessee Titans 13 to 3 that night and we had a wonderful time.

By the time the game was over, and we got out of the stadium, all the restaurants were closed. So, Sherri and I went back to the hotel. Even though it was late, we decided to explore our enormous hotel. After walking around, we realized that all the restaurants inside the hotel were also closed. We finally went back to our room and just made do with what we had with us. So, we sat out on the balcony and had peanut butter and bananas. As anyone can tell, we are very high maintenance. Ha!

Sherri loves a country breakfast so the next morning, I treated her to breakfast at Bob Evans. I must say that breakfast is the only thing that Bob Evans serves that I will eat but it was good, and I knew it would make Sherri happy. She loved it.

After Breakfast it was time to point our car north and head towards Shepherdsville. Since it was the beginning of a long Labor Day weekend, it seemed only fitting to listen to the fun music of Jimmy Buffet during our drive home. I loved it!

On the way home, we stopped at Bright's Antique Mall in Franklin Ky to look around. I bought an old Walton's Christmas album because we love that kind of stuff, then it was back on the road again.

We got home just before 3:00 Friday afternoon and Sherri had to go to sleep as she had to work that night.

Since it was Labor Day weekend, we decided to let the relaxing feeling of our little trip extend throughout the rest of the weekend. So, on Saturday we grilled steaks and watched a Jimmy Buffet concert on TV. The next day we were invited to a cookout at Jerry and Denise's. We had a wonderful time. It was a great way to end our nice relaxing vacation weekend. A vacation is all about relaxing and doing what you enjoy. After the summer we've had, it was wonderful to do just that. Life is good.

A House of Memories

There can be a lot of good that comes from living in the same home for most of your life, but there can also be some bad as well. The good is that you grow up learning the importance of community. By doing so, you learn to coexist comfortably with your neighbors, even though it might be difficult at times. During the 1970's, I grew up in a subdivision and I chose to stay there. Our neighbors almost became a second family, albeit complete with all the color and dysfunction that can appear in any extended family. As time went by and my siblings moved out, I noticed that I even saw my neighbors more often then I saw some of my family members. I was fortunate to grow up in a new middle-class subdivision. I was surrounded by good, honest, responsible people that showed by example the importance of working hard and taking care of their families and their homes. As I grew older, I learned how to take care of that same home that I was blessed to grow up in.

For me, the saddest thing about staying in the subdivision I grew up in was that after living there for decades, my longtime neighbors began to slowly pass away. It was quite emotional for me because I had known these neighbors since I was a small child and as I said, they felt kind of like extended family. Many of them were close personal friends of my parents years ago, so there were a lot of emotional layers to why it made me sad. There is actually a grieving process that occurs while watching your old neighborhood slowly decay and die away.

On top of that, I also noticed that staying in the same subdivision over a long period of time, many of the homes that were once new had become old. As the years go by the older homes are less desirable to young families and that in turn makes them more susceptible to becoming rental homes. It's usually not a good idea to have rental property in your neighborhood. As my wife can attest, seeing my reaction to these changes

has also been rather emotional for me. Life is all about change, so it's best
to just allow yourself to adjust and move forward.

The reason I never moved away from my home is rather complex. My disability makes my situation much different than most other people. I've always had to live within the confines of my handicap. Because of living on social security disability, that also meant financially as well. Staying in the home I grew up in was just a smarter move for me financially, so I stayed put. Plus, as you can tell, I love my home and I feel truly blessed to have it.

The book started with a group of stories that centered around this same old house that my parents bought for their family during the summer of 1967. Back then, the house was newly built. That has now been more than a half a century ago. At the time, I was just 3 years old. In all those years, a lot of things have changed, but one thing has remained the same. I still live in that same house with my wife. It has slowly evolved over the years. Without ever moving, the address on the house changed from Riverview Drive to Riverview Lane. Built in 1965, the house was less than 1400 square feet. It had 3 bedrooms and a full basement. In a short amount of time, my parents made the house a home. Somehow, my parents, along with their four children managed to coexist comfortably with just one bathroom. Doing so, takes a lot of preplanning, patience and teamwork. A family of 6 doing that in this day and age, is virtually unthinkable.

The house has been many things to many people. While growing up, it's where my friends and I hung out on cold winter days and where we camped out on hot summer nights. To my parents' grandchildren, this was Papa's house, Nana's house or Mamaw's house. More than 35 years later, my nephew Demian's tiny footprints are fading but still visible in the sidewalk, near the backdoor. My brother Jerry's initials are preserved on the cement wall in the basement. In the 1970's, my parents had the side porch made into a small den. Shortly thereafter, my dad had the driveway blacktopped. In the early 80's, he had a 2-car garage built and added a patio out back. In 1998, I had the basement entrance enclosed with lattice board. The old house was modernized in 2005 when central air was installed. Up to that point, the house was cooled with window air conditioners. A year later, I landscaped the yard by planting multiple trees, bushes and flowers. Then, I added creek rock and steppingstones for decoration. Mom loved it so much that she called it "The Garden".

I would say without question that the most iconic thing associated with the Huckaby house is the grandfather clock that proudly stands in the corner of the living room. The story goes that while serving in the Army and stationed in Germany, my dad purchased the old antique grandfather clock from a German by merely giving him a carton of American cigarettes. After a brief stay in Fort Riley Kansas, the clock was moved with the family to its Kentucky home, where it currently resides. The beautiful old clock has become so synonymous with the Huckaby house because it's been the backdrop of hundreds, if not thousands of family pictures over the years. It has presided over every single Christmas gathering in the house for more than a half a century.

There are also three other things in the house that carry a lot of sentimental value. One is the antique coo coo clock that my dad sent my mom while he was in Korea. The other is the old mantle clock that had belonged to my Aunt Rose. It rests on the fireplace mantel in the living room. Just above the old clock hangs a beautifully framed, pastel drawing of Sherri's grandfather. These are the kinds of family artifacts that help a house become a home.

The old home place has a lot of family history. Over the years, my mom entertained everything from Cub Scout meetings, bunco parties, wedding showers, baby showers and prayer meetings, not to mention, she hosted countless Thanksgiving and Christmas dinners at the house. All throughout my childhood, we always met around the kitchen table as a family and had supper together.

In 2008, a few friends helped me to remove the wallpaper from the bathroom and strip and stain the vanity. The following year, we remodeled the kitchen by refinishing the cabinets, replacing the countertop, stripping off the wallpaper and repainting the walls.

Sherri and I married in the spring of 2015. Since then, she has brought a great deal of care and warmth to the old house. During that time, the house felt as though it had been reborn. It no longer looked or felt like my parents' house. That doesn't mean it's better, it just means it's different. Sherri and I have made the old house our own. There is enough stress and tension in this world, so we wanted our home to have a very relaxing and peaceful feel to it. We have a cat that is eager to greet you at the door. We have beautiful back yard that's very welcoming to all of our friends and neighbors alike. It's great for hosting cookouts and family gatherings. Sherri and I love our home year-round, but none more so then winter. There is nowhere that Sherri and I would rather be on a cold winter night then home in front of the fireplace. During the Christmas holiday season, we decorate our home with lots of family tradition and fun nostalgia.

Throughout the years, the old house has seen a lot of good times and bad times. My mom and Hal died at the house. I accepted Christ at the house, and Sherri and I were married at the house. I guess you could say the house kind of chronicles the story of a simple, blue collar American family. The house has provided a backdrop for a lifetime of wonderful memories. It has also provided a fortress of strength during the storms of life. To other people, it might just seem like any other house, but to me, it's the only home I've ever known. There is an old saying that says, "home is where the heart is", and I would say that is true. As I have gotten older, I've come to realize that it's important to give thanks for the simple pleasures in life. I am truly grateful. Growing up in this modest home has given me what most people only dream of, a lifetime of simple pleasures and positive memories. They say, "you can't go home again". Well, I know I can never go back to the way my house was as a child, but I still live in the old home place and it's still where my heart calls home. I am grateful to God that He gave me the opportunity of owning my childhood home. I feel blessed to just be living a simple man's American dream. God is so good.

Made in USA - North Chelmsford, MA
1113387_9780578523491
05.21.2020 0852